DATE DUE	

PERFECT
PORCHES

PERFECT
PORCHES

Designing Welcoming Spaces for Outdoor Living

Paula S. Wallace

With photographs by Chia Chong and Adam Kuehl

CLARKSON POTTER/PUBLISHERS
NEW YORK

Contents

Waterfront Porches

Country Porches

Creating Porch Rooms

Design Directory

Index

Introduction

A good porch is a dear and treasured friend. It holds on to family secrets, keeping them safely hidden in nooks and crannies until it's time for them to be revealed. A porch invites lively celebration, a chance to let loose, to sing, to dance, to be free. It can also encourage reflection and afford the rare opportunity to be still.

Porches provide a passageway between our public and personal lives. Mine is the first thing I see when I return home, and it unfailingly gives me a welcoming greeting: the brilliant red roses, the quiet murmur of the fountain, the balmy and aromatic herbs in terra-cotta pots that hang from a vintage wrought-iron planter. This side porch is a private, sensual world that helps me to recall a childhood filled with warm memories. I remember playing house under card tables cloaked in vintage tablecloths on my parents' porch in Atlanta when I was younger, my sister and I pretending to be Laura and Mary Ingalls. Other times, I would sit tucked beside my father on a glider as he listened to baseball games on the radio.

Even in large, institutional settings, porches can create a sense of family and community; they're vital components of the environment at the Georgia campuses of the Savannah College of Art and Design (SCAD), where I serve as president. At Smithfield Cottage, graduate students sit on the wicker swing and muse over thesis ideas. At Magnolia Hall, university guests laze on rockers

The side porch of Lai Wa Hall (left) and the front porch of Magnolia Hall (opposite) are but two examples of the inviting outdoor rooms across SCAD's Savannah campus.

and watch processions of wedding parties and hurried walkers in Forsyth Park. Across the park is Lai Wa Hall, where visitors can relax on a side porch with mirrors, candled sconces and rockers that look out onto the park's grand fountain and wide green lawns.

An iconic part of our nation's cultural history, the porch has been immortalized by painters including Winslow Homer, Edward Hopper and Norman Rockwell. Porches provide the setting in literary works such as Harper Lee's *To Kill a Mockingbird* and Arthur Miller's *All My Sons*. Mark Twain's porch in Hartford, Connecticut, doubled as his study. When Eudora Welty started to earn money from her stories, she used some of it to screen in her back porch in Jackson, Mississippi.

These outdoor living rooms have been witnesses to our political history, too. Abraham Lincoln played checkers with his son Tad on the back porch at the Soldiers' Home in Washington, D.C., where the family resided during the summers of the Civil War; their view looked onto the Washington Monument's and Capitol dome's constructions. Theodore Roosevelt was on his Cove Neck, New York, porch in 1904 when he was asked to be the Republican Party's presidential candidate; throughout his term he entertained ambassadors as well as suffragettes and Olympic athletes on its decking.

Architecturally, a porch is nothing more than a roofed exterior that shares a common wall with the house, but its stylistic interpretations are vast: there are verandas and porticos and loggias; there are side porches, back porches and front porches. No matter where they were positioned, porches remained a prominent fixture of American architecture for centuries, at least until World War II, when they teetered on the edge of obsolescence. The blame likely rested with the advent of television, air-conditioning and ranch home design, which demoted porches to mere covered entryways.

But during the past several decades, porches have entered a modern renaissance—and not a moment too soon. With overscheduled lives, we yearn for time to connect and relax. Families gather around

BELOW: A romantic glow is cast across Paula and Taras Danyluk's waterfront porch.

fire pits, couples cook outside in summer kitchens. Wide porches provide space for children to play and adults to nap. Whatever their form or dimensions, they help us to rely less on artificial temperatures and more on natural cooling elements such as mild breezes, handheld fans and the South's oldest antidote for global warming: sweet iced tea.

The porch is a domestic stage—a carefully crafted theater set where we are both audience and performer. As audiences, we witness nature's rhythms: we applaud as spring blossoms and autumn leaves dance, as birds preen and nest, and as the sun and moon light our lawns. The porch allows us to people-watch, sheltered from the entanglements of interaction, if we wish, or close enough to call out a greeting. For my mother and, I imagine, others like her who are no longer able to get out much, the porch offers an expansion of their world—a change of scenery and a connection to the busyness of daily life and to the characters who populate it.

As in all theaters, set design is vital, so how does one create a comfortable, stylish and inviting porch? While considering the impact of sun, rain and wind we strive to create atmospheres that are akin to those of our interior rooms—only hardier. Vero Beach, Florida, architect Clem Schaub describes his designs as "living porches" where the dimensions and features are similar to those inside, including conversational seating arrangements and fireplaces. Today's porches are wider and more colorful than their predecessors; they incorporate more all-weather furnishings and alternative flooring solutions. All of these elements work together to form an inviting area for a quiet read with a cup of coffee or a

Fresh flowers bridge the space between interior rooms and gardens and add bursts of color to a porch. A mason jar at the Danyluk home in Savannah, Georgia, holds bright pink limonium (above); hand-turned maple vases are filled with wild apples, burning bush and late-season okra at the Martin home in Waco, Kentucky (middle); and tiger lilies, Queen Anne's lace and butterfly bush grace a Nantucket basket at the Carroll home on Martha's Vineyard, Massachusetts.

boisterous party with stronger beverages. From dawn until dusk and beyond, a comfortable and well-designed porch percolates infinite hours of pleasure.

Objects that bring comfort and delight inside the house can be reimagined to work outside, too. Vases bursting with lush, fresh flowers from the garden add color and scent, while pillows cushion wicker, swings and hammocks. Lamps, kerosene lanterns and candles sprinkled about can create a flattering glow and dramatic shadows and enable evening reading and game playing.

Furnishings offer more than just seating and illumination; they also express the owners' personalities. The sleek blue-green mosaic tile table and teak lounges of Eleanore and Domenico De Sole's modern Hilton Head Island, South Carolina, beach house set a different mood than the vintage painted wooden chest of drawers and delicate iron table of Katherine Sandoz and Daniel Bucey's cypress bungalow in Savannah, Georgia. Custom-made seating like the snowshoe chairs at Jane McDill Smith's Charles Platt–designed home in Woodstock, Vermont, is a wonderful choice that reflects the home's environs and the family's activities. All of these alchemies of personal style instantly identify a porch with its residents.

An imaginative use of decorative objects truly sets a porch apart and further extends the idea of the space as an outdoor room. Where porches used to be filled merely with functional furniture, many now include works of art. While one might hesitate

ABOVE: Ostrich eggs and spheres made from rope and canvas strips add texture and curves to the angular lines of the Van Asperen home in St. Helena, California.

CENTER: An antique oar, a Victorian urn filled with coral and conch shells, and white tin fish are the nautical motifs on the Key West, Florida, porch of designer Michael Pelkey.

LEFT: A rough-hewn bench and aboriginal artwork complement the untreated eucalyptus log exterior of the guest cabin at the DeHennis home in Glen Ellen, California.

to incorporate original pieces that may seem too fragile for the outside, many forms, including sculptural works, can be displayed without concern about damage—in fact, weathering can enhance the beauty and mystique of some pieces. A roughly chiseled granite sculpture by Jesús Moroles is in harmony with its wooded riverside surroundings at Arthur Roger's home in Poplarville, Mississippi, while an aboriginal work complements the Australia-inspired architecture of Linda and Tommy DeHennis's Glen Ellen, California, home. At the Neshoba County Fair in Philadelphia, Mississippi, the walls themselves become canvases; families paint all matter of colorful designs directly onto the cabins.

Perfect Porches features forty homes from myriad landscapes: the polychromatic porches of a historic coastal village in Massachusetts, a two-story screened porch on a thoroughbred farm in Kentucky, a creekside hacienda porch at a ranch in Texas, a traditional Craftsman cottage's porch overlooking San Francisco's harbor and many, many more. Each illustrates our country's broad architectural and geographical range. On the Gulf Coast, porches need extended eaves to protect from the diluvial rains. In hotter climes, porches benefit from cool tile floors. In areas prone to biting insects, porches need screens; in some urban areas, porches need screens not for mosquitoes but for privacy. Along the way you'll read about the owners' approaches to decorative challenges as well as their stories of meeting their spouses, encountering ghosts and singing arias, all on their porches.

Porches engage the senses: the sight of beloved neighbors, the scent of fresh-cut grass, the sound of rain on the roof, the comforting warmth of a quilt, the taste of cold lemonade, the reassuring undulations of a grandmother's rocking chair. Whether bejeweled with ornamental woodwork and furnishings or striking in their simplicity, these outdoor rooms are vital to our communities, our families—and ourselves.

BELOW: Snowshoe chairs at the Charles Platt-designed PineApple Hill home of Jane McDill Smith are an inventive seating solution that reflect the family's active lifestyle as well as the Vermont landscape.

COASTAL
PORCHES

One of a pair of carved gates made by David Merrill, a former industrial arts teacher at Central Connecticut State University, offers privacy while also hiding unused chairs and beach equipment at this home on Martha's Vineyard, Massachusetts.

Grand Illumination

OAK BLUFFS, MASSACHUSETTS

For one evening each August, the nineteenth-century village of Oak Bluffs on the island of Martha's Vineyard is transformed by thousands of candlelit Asian lanterns hung from the eaves of cottage porches. The result is a brief but magical experience—akin to the flowering of a rare orchid, according to former Martha's Vineyard Campmeeting Association board member John Goldthwait. The festivities represent the best that a porch-centered community can offer—soft chatter, peals of laughter, candlelight and old-fashioned family fun.

This thriving coastal "city in the woods" was founded as a spiritual retreat on a half acre of sheep pasture in 1835. As organized religion loosened up following the Second Great Awakening, the area began to draw more than the Methodists who originally pitched six family-sized canvas tents on wooden platforms, gathering for revivals in this idyllic spot beneath the oak grove's arching limbs. Eventually 450 four-room Carpenter Gothic cottages were raised along streets that were sometimes named for congregations, like Fourth Street Avenue, in honor of the Fourth Street Methodist Church in New Bedford, the nearest city on the

LEFT: A home owner lights a silk lantern that has witnessed more than a hundred Grand Illuminations. Lanterns are fragile creatures that need tender loving care—and occasional repairs. For the paper variety, a mixture of rice paper and egg whites is used for patching.

OPPOSITE: Paper parasols flanking a walkway extend the Asian theme.

LEFT: The cottages have always been polychrome, but were originally earth-toned, as seen here at the home of Susan and Larry Zielinski.

BELOW: The double doors throughout Oak Bluffs harken back to flapped tent openings and church doors.

PRECEDING PAGES: Grand Illumination attracts thousands of admirers each year.

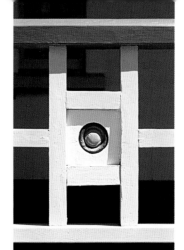

Massachusetts mainland. Built from inexpensive Southern yellow pine brought up north following the Civil War, the fanciful cottages feature arched windows and steeply gabled roofs that were inspired by Gothic cathedrals. They are decorated with lacy gingerbread trimmings and dado saw-cut railings, much of which was made on the island at the local fretwork mill. The "stressed skin" construction—essentially one thin, uninsulated layer of vertical tongue-and-groove boards between four posts that give the houses their stability—was originally assembled on top of platforms, just as the tents were.

These railinged decks were at first uncovered, then covered with awnings; it wasn't until the 1880s that the roofs began to be added, sheltering the outside living areas and thus making them true porches. In this Victorian era, the formalities of society were such that approaching and entering a house had many conventions, including offering calling cards and being greeted in the foyer before being welcomed into a parlor. But in Oak Bluffs, the porch was, and is, an informal sitting room for entertaining guests, given the modest dimensions of the homes themselves and the prevailing atmosphere of neighborly exchanges.

About three hundred of the cottages remain across 34 acres. While often wildly colored, much like the Painted Ladies of San Francisco, with bright pinks, blues and oranges, they were originally of modest hues. "The cottages were always polychrome," according to architect and local historian Doug Ulwick, "but less vibrantly so, in earth tones including beige, brown and dark green."

Except for that final Wednesday evening of the summer season, that is, when the colorful lanterns light up the night with

RIGHT: Much of the decorative woodwork known as "gingerbread" was made on the island at the local fretwork mill. In these examples, decorative railings and a fleur-de-lis privacy rope add color and interest.

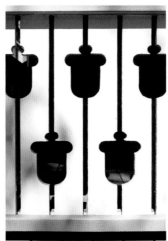

their roses, flags and birds. No one really owns them, any more than they own the oak trees or the land itself (which is leased), but they are so much a part of the community that they ritually pass from one cottage owner to the next.

Most of the lanterns are painted rice paper on collapsible metal frames, although some of greater value are silk, which is frayed and thin in spots but still graced with wonderful period illustrations. On the morning before the chosen night in August, many lanterns are seen newly emerged from their boxes, airing in their flattened state because tradition holds that home owners should not hang them on their houses until after noon. Meanwhile, boxes and tins of candle stubs from the previous year's celebration are remelted into rinsed tuna cans and rigged into the lantern frames.

The festivities begin inside the 1879 Tabernacle, which serves as the community's hub. The rigid wrought-iron structure radiates from a forty-foot mast, sheltering some 2,500 celebrants on Grand Illumination night as well as the more modest crowds that

attend events throughout the summer season. Initiated in 1869 to attract buyers to properties between the campground and the sea, Grand Illumination night has come to include a performance by the Vineyard Haven Band. As many as 10,000 guests inside and around the Tabernacle have raised their voices as one in songs like "I'm in the Swiss Navy," "Amazing Grace" and "Home on the Range."

Once the lights are dimmed and the room is hushed following the last song, a master of ceremonies walks onstage to offer a few words and introduce a community elder charged with lighting the first candle. This single flame sparks all of the lanterns inside the Tabernacle, and they in turn signal residents of the grove to illuminate their porches, which surround the Tabernacle's grounds. Soon enough the whole village is warmed by soft golden light, but a glow also radiates from visitors and community members coming together for a wholesome ritual that is blessedly free of any commercial elements. Perhaps resident Susan Weldon says it best: "It happens so quickly…and ends so quickly…I'd believe you if you said it was a dream."

ABOVE LEFT: A toy dinosaur takes a ride in a lantern shaped as a hot air balloon that's painted with prehistoric scenes.

ABOVE RIGHT: An unpainted lantern, hung from decorative woodwork that includes an "eyebrow" over an arched window, casts moody red light.

OPPOSITE, LEFT: Sisters Kyla and Caitlyn McCartney began their lemonade business twenty years ago a stone's throw from their grandparents' porch. Their proceeds are donated to the restoration of the Tabernacle, which is within sight of the stand. Their golden retriever, Watson, enjoys his place of honor.

OPPOSITE, RIGHT: On the morning of Grand Illumination, families air out the lanterns in the sun.

A Gulf Coast Rain Porch

GAIL AND RALPH REYNOLDS — POINT CLEAR, ALABAMA

When Ralph Reynolds was coming up in Alabama (as they say in the South), he helped his father with his roofing business near Mobile Bay in the summers. It was brutal work, with boiling tar, burning sun, drenching humidity and biting insects. But every now and again a job at Point Clear would come along, and the pair could at least enjoy the cooling breezes and view of the waterfront, the most sought-after address in the area. "For as long as I can remember, I've always wanted a house along that boardwalk," Ralph recalls.

One of the many roofs that Ralph Sr. and Ralph Jr. repaired was that of the Burke-Herndon home, which is among the grandest along the mile-wide historic district. Impressive with its Queen Anne–style grace and proportions, the raised cottage also has a feature that is particular to the Gulf Coast—a rain porch designed to withstand the annual sixty-five-inch inundation delivered to this, the wettest part of the country. Extreme conditions called for inventive solutions. Because the summer storms blow off the bay every afternoon with often horizontal rains, a standard eave's

LEFT: The original rippling glass panes of the two-over-two double-hung windows were part of the 15,000-piece salvage effort for this historic 1881 house.

OPPOSITE: Deep Scalamandré-covered cushions on McGuire wicker seating offer comfortable perches from which to enjoy the pageant provided by Mobile Bay's weather, ships and visitors. The oyster shell lamp is from Crocker Antiques and Garden.

BELOW: Cast-iron "shutter dogs" hold back the louvered shutters.

BOTTOM: The salvaged columns flanking the doorway, from Crocker Antiques and Garden, are inventive planters. The gas lamps are from Bevolo Gas Lights in New Orleans.

RIGHT: The curved "hips" of the pine-shake roof are one of the elegant and defining features of this rain porch. The eight-foot eave extension is supported by columns on brick piers, which prevent rot and termite infestation.

pitch and depth won't suffice; a rain porch extends an additional six to eight feet toward the lawn. The Burke-Herndon roof is an especially elegant example of this accommodation, with a curved "hip" construction rather than sides that meet at hard angles. "In the space of an hour on a sweltering day, a blue sky can fill up with pitch-black or even green clouds that bring on a violent—but cooling—drenching. It's an exciting experience; our extra eight feet of eaves provide safe cover for the performance in even the worst blows," Ralph explains.

Ralph and his wife, Gail, purchased the property in 2001. While it fulfilled a childhood dream for him, the couple knew they had a formidable renovation project ahead that they would have to manage from their homes in the Northeast. They hired the local firm of Walcott Adams Verneuille Architects along with builders Randy and Eric Crocker, all of whom had significant experience with historic local structures. The two-year deconstruction and redesign resulted in a light-filled interior encased in the ornate shell of a Queen Anne silhouette, all behind the defining bay-front façade. The balance between old and new was a delicate one for all concerned. In project architect Lea Verneuille's words, "In cases like this, you naturally feel a great responsibility to the client and to the community, but also to the house itself—to honor and give them all your best work."

The desire to reuse the existing structure's materials meant that 15,000 individual pieces had to be numbered and stored in a custom-built garage that would protect them from the elements and keep them organized. Everything from doorknobs to porch decking to window weights was salvaged; in the end, 90 percent of the old house was repurposed into the new. Thanks to a surgical demolition, the Crocker team discovered some important architectural history, including the roof's original covering. Buried underneath layers of asphalt shingles was a small section of the original wooden shakes, so the decision was made to restore all of the home's roofs to treated pine. Not only is this a more attractive—and historically appropriate—solution than asphalt,

BELOW: While known as the Burke-Herndon home, on the boardwalk side of the lawn a brass sign gives Ralph's moniker for it: Long Gamma, which is a reference to the investment strategy that made the purchase—and restoration—of the house possible.

OPPOSITE: The view from the bay hall across the porch and lawn to the two-story pier.

but "the way the shakes are lapped, nailed and felted makes them resistant to even hurricane force winds," Randy explains.

Most of the porch was salvaged, including the tongue-and-groove decking, bead-board ceiling, balusters, beams and the pairs of operable louvered shutters with their cast-iron "shutter dogs" that frame the full-length double-hung windows. The windows with their atmospheric rippling vintage glass allow walk-through access to the porch from the living room.

Immersed in this history, Ralph and Gail, along with their children and guests, can gaze out to the bay the Spanish called Bahía del Espíritu Santo (the Bay of the Holy Spirit) from comfortable, oversized wicker seating. There's always something to watch, from shrimpers on the water to the rolling clouds to people strolling along the boardwalk that was once used for wagons carrying the day's catch. In the evenings, driftwood bonfires light up the private beach while cicadas chirp their lullabies.

It's been many moons since Ralph was up on the roof rather than relaxing beneath it; his life's journey continues at least part of the year here where he was formed, and now his children are learning to fish, crab and experience Southern living, too. His father approves of the roof's return to its original glory, and that is an added bonus.

BELOW: The private piers of the Point Clear historic district are silhouetted against the setting sun.

OPPOSITE: The welcoming lights of the Reynolds home beckon across the pier that spans their private beach. On calm evenings, driftwood bonfires provide additional light and drama.

A Lowcountry Porch

ELEANORE AND DOMENICO DE SOLE — HILTON HEAD ISLAND,
SOUTH CAROLINA

For two people who love nothing more than sailing the open seas, the next best thing on dry land is a tailored Carolina house with the Atlantic as the front lawn and a Caribbean-blue lap pool just steps away from the interior. The sun's rays skim the pool's surface, casting ripples across Eleanore and Domenico De Sole's contemporary home and its adjoining porch on Hilton Head Island, immersing all of the living spaces in shimmering light.

Although a native of Washington, D.C., Eleanore began visiting the island when her parents built a vacation home nearby. She shared her love of the place with her husband, Domenico, the former chairman and CEO of Gucci Group, who had spent his childhood summers in southern Italy where he developed his kindred love of coastal places. In 1996, the couple purchased a beach house that, while ideally situated, lacked the space and comfort expected in a year-round residence. As they envisioned a new home on the existing lot, outdoor living was near the top of their agenda. "We designed the porch as a separate haven," says Eleanore of this vital component of their twenty-seven-month collaboration with Thomas & Denzinger Architects.

LEFT: A tabby wall and small high windows behind the sofa frame the views of the palm trees while also maintaining a sense of privacy.

OPPOSITE: Outdoor fabrics by John Hutton and Donghia in soft colors were chosen to reflect the surrounding flora, beach grasses, ocean and pool. The teak seating is by Sutherland.

Contractor Kraig Minckler skinned the rear wall of the porch using tabby, a traditional, highly textured Lowcountry treatment that combines local oyster shells and cement. Small square windows high in the wall maintain privacy from the neighbors while offering small-aperture views of rustling palm fronds. "The windows promote the idea of breeziness without distracting from the main view toward the pool and ocean," explains designer Tom Scheerer. Since the other three sides of the porch are essentially open, screens keep things livable at times when insects would otherwise chase everyone indoors. "We knew we wanted to enjoy the porch at dusk, when mosquitoes and no-see-ums—our tiny but pesky gnats—are at their peak," Eleanore explains. The open construction also allows for the optimal flow of air off the water on those hot Southern nights.

Views of the dunes and ocean are framed by Japanese black pine and palmetto trees and accented by sculptural works selected by the couple, who are avid modern art collectors. The subtle seaside theme continues with details like the aqueous blue and green glass mosaic tiles arranged by craftsman Charles Ramberg atop a custom coffee table by Scheerer. To foster the idea of relaxation and informality, the designer explains, the adjacent seating by Sutherland is lower and "loungier" than elsewhere on the property.

The sea is also present in the choice of teak for the chairs, since that species is employed by shipwrights. Flanking a sofa designed by Scheerer, twin floor lamps have unlacquered copper-and-brass bases in a triangular shape that enhances stability against ocean winds. Whipstitched seams on the lamps' durable faux-parchment lamp shades promote the feeling of a no-fuss living room, while the custom-designed all-weather Sacco carpet underfoot completes the scene with warmth and intimacy and resists damage from the elements. A brass ship's bell with a rope-knot handle attached to a post next to the porch calls guests for dinner from the dunes below.

The porch, in all, has a kind of marine simplicity—a flow of clean lines, color and texture provided by furnishings and surfaces that are as stylish and worry-free as those of a fine sailboat. Surf sounds and brisk breezes transform this porch into a vessel, its sitters into the crew.

OPPOSITE: A ship's bell rings out to friends and family who are enjoying the sea, alerting them to phone calls or meals. Shrimp boats with their outstretched green net wings travel past throughout most of the year.

BELOW: *Marathon Man* by Larry Young takes to the dunes near the lap pool.

LEFT: The architectural firm of Thomas & Denzinger, builder Kraig Minckler and interior designer Tom Scheerer are the team behind the realization of the De Soles' vision for their home.

A Mediterranean Revival Loggia

PEGGY AND DUDLEY MOORE — PALM BEACH, FLORIDA

Behind a twelve-foot ficus hedge in the historic Estate section of this legendary beachfront community sits a villa as whimsical as it is grand. Famed Florida architect John L. Volk, who created many of the iconic storefronts on the city's tony Worth Avenue, also employed his signature Mediterranean Revival style in this 1927 residence. Seven decades later, it underwent an extensive restoration orchestrated by Smith Architectural Group. The finishing touches were added by Margaret Moore Chambers, who styled the spectacular L-shaped loggia for her parents, Peggy and Dudley Moore, to bridge the lush interiors she created to the verdant Mediterranean-themed garden and grounds designed by Mario Nievera.

Beneath the new coffered-cypress ceiling (which was dropped to accommodate air-conditioning units for the interior), the loggia is illuminated with Spanish wrought-iron pendants that reinforce the Mediterranean look. Davis General Contracting was responsible for the modern extension to the loggia that doubled

LEFT: Majolica flowers hung on the walls lining the 100-foot-long loggia add color and enhance the Mediterranean mood. "They're so cheerful," says Peggy, "just like an Easter basket!"

OPPOSITE: The coffered-cypress ceiling helps to create the impression of an outdoor room. The chairs are by Bielecky Brothers; the fabric is by Bassett McNab. Retractable shades descend from the arches, offering protection from sun and storms.

the amount of sheltered living space for the family without interrupting the purity of the period statement. The care taken with the redesign was honored with the Preservation Foundation of Palm Beach's Ballinger Award for excellence, and the house was also awarded landmark status.

Updated conveniences were not sacrificed in the process, however. The floor needed replacing, since the original Cuban tiles could not be found in sufficient quantities for the renovation. Now four generations of the family live outdoors throughout the year, thanks in part to radiant heating buried beneath the honed limestone tiles. And, whenever the sun is out, the off-white stone reflects light onto the ceilings and vibrantly painted walls.

One of Margaret's biggest design challenges was making the 100-foot-long, 10-foot-high expanse accessible and lounge-friendly with comfortable furnishings that wouldn't languish in the vast space. Bielecky Brothers chairs and vintage wicker seating paired with bombé chests and occasional tables beckon in the airy loggia. Her parents adore the bright warm color she chose for the classic Bassett McNab fabric on the seating. "The quality of the sunlight varies, so we went with a happy apricot shade that stayed true day and night and complemented the walls," she says. Concealed steel hurricane shades can be rolled down to close each of the arches, shielding and preserving fragile furnishings from the elements. The screens also offer shade from the summer sun and block winter winds.

Peggy's ninety-four-year-old mother knits in a favorite chair with a view of the pool, and the grandchildren play in the loggia when it rains. But this rose-colored enclave is as suited to benefit concerts by visiting tenors as it is to family time. Consummate hosts of intimate gatherings and lavish public affairs alike, the family entertain frequently as part of their deep commitment to local causes, including the Society of the Four Arts and the Preservation Foundation.

That commitment extends to decorative accents supplied by artisans. "We tried to bring the garden into the loggia with the flowers," says Chambers, referring to the extensive display of majolica and Pallisey ceramics that enliven the walls. "The ceramic reptiles are a reminder of how much the children enjoy

chasing lizards around." Recalling nature, too, are vintage seashell-encrusted mirrors and lamps.

Mario Nievera extended the property's Mediterranean ocean-front theme by planting grapefruit, honeybell and lemon and lime trees and by snuggling garden walls in a cloak of magenta bougainvillea. But there is far more to his landscape design than its cultural associations. Recognizing that this is a primary residence for the Moores, his work slowly evolves throughout the year in exquisite form, color and scent. "Peggy always pushed me to develop elegant designs in the landscape," Mario notes, "so the pavings and flower-filled planting beds are intricately patterned." Down to the newly planted Canary Island date palms with fronds fluttering against the cerulean sky, true grandeur has been revived at this Palm Beach jewel.

ABOVE: The loggia and courtyard are perfect areas for entertaining or enjoying quiet family evenings. Dudley helped design the pool for the grandchildren, including umbrellas that can be inserted into the pool's floor to protect them from the sun, and a larger shallow area that is decorated with sea life mosaics.

OPPOSITE, ABOVE: Petal-edged vintage wicker forms a conversational area at one end of the L-shaped loggia. The wrought-iron pendant lamps were created based on an antique model.

OPPOSITE, BELOW: The deep green glazes of Pallisey plates and platters complement the pink stucco walls while adding a sense of whimsy with their fanciful creatures.

A Poolside Pavilion

MELINDA AND RICK SCHAUB — VERO BEACH, FLORIDA

When the eight Schaub children were growing up in their house on the shore of Lake Michigan, they could race from the porch down steep wooden steps to the beach below. Their view of the water—and having the lake as a playground, temperatures allowing—was a rare year-round gift. Little did oldest brothers Rick and Clem know that many decades later they would join forces to design Rick's winter home in Vero Beach, Florida. Instead of a porch on a lake, however, they would create one alongside an elegant sweep of a pool that reflects the tropical plants and modern Caribbean-influenced architecture of the exclusive Windsor community.

Outdoor living is a foundation value in Windsor, where golfing, riding, swimming, shooting and playing tennis are all regular parts of life. Rick and his wife, Melinda, purchased adjoining lots with the intent of creating their own village of buildings around a central lawn, playing on the tropical islands' design of courtyard

LEFT: Espresso-stained coconut husk containers from Andrianna Shamaris's New York gallery and the orange Tempo side table by Prospero Rasulo add punches of color and weight to the airy monochromatic pavilion. A cast stone Herpel floor with a sand texture reinforces the island feel.

OPPOSITE: Caribbean houses were designed to optimize outdoor living before the advent of air-conditioning; in Vero Beach, the Schaubs designed their residence and guest cottage around a central lawn and pool and oriented the buildings to block wind, welcome breezes, shield them from the sun in the summer and welcome it during the winter.

houses, where rooms are oriented around the outdoor space. Clem, an architect who has been involved with the community since its founding in the 1990s, collaborated with them to create a tin-roofed stucco-over-cement-block-construction residence and guest cottage designed to divert the north wind, embrace the sun, welcome breezes and offer ample opportunities to appreciate all of the surrounding beauty.

The cottage features what Clem calls a "living porch"—a space of room-sized dimensions that can accommodate furniture arranged in conversational areas and elements traditionally reserved for interiors, including fireplaces and showers. Here, the painted brick fireplace radiates warmth on nippy evenings and frames collections of succulents during the summer months. From the sleek white chairs, sofa and lounges in this sheltered space, guests can look across to the residence's living room, which, courtesy of ingenious concealed-frame floor-to-ceiling sliding glass doors, is more like a glazed porch. "I blocked in the curving pool connecting the guesthouse and residence on big sheets of paper with colored markers," says Rick. "As with all of our projects, Clem and I collaborated on the overall schematics but he ran with it from there." Clem counters, "Rick was definitely a broad-stroke man in the deal, but he had a real feel for the way the buildings would communicate." Brothers working closely together might occasionally find themselves at odds, so they built an arbitration

ABOVE AND CENTER: In the warmer months, succulents take the place of logs in the brick fireplace.

RIGHT: Even unlit, orange square hurricane lamps are vibrant accent pieces.

OPPOSITE: Philippe Starck side tables and ultrathin chaise lounges are stylish and functional but don't block the view from the seating area behind them. The white furniture also looks dynamic against the dense clipped lawn when more sun is desired.

clause into their contract. "If we argued, our mother settled things between us!" Rick laughs.

The guest cottage, with its own street-side entrance, can be a private oasis, yet it's in a kind of conversation with the house across the stretch of the Atlantic-colored pool. Nestled under the second floor of the cottage next to the pool is the pavilion. "It's really a combination of a cabana and a guesthouse," Clem says, "so it gets a lot of use in season." An outdoor shower and changing areas just inside encourage that poolside function.

ABOVE: Windsor's architecture is a modern interpretation of British Colonial island design, where the cottage silhouette was amended to include "rafter tails," or extended eaves, to keep rain away from foundations, windows and doors. With the absence of decks and the darker coloring that reflects the surrounding architecture and plants, the pool looks more like a pond in the grass.

OPPOSITE: The stepping-stones across the pool are like little islands that encourage an interaction with the water.

"I'm a porch freak in general," Clem confesses. "Sometimes with my designs, it's more like a house attached to the porch—they're that large and that vital, with exposed staircases, external foyers and even full kitchens. If you design a porch to have true room dimensions to accommodate people sitting eye to eye rather than lined up as if on the deck of a ship, you'll naturally use that space more, gravitate toward it." Here at his brother's house, that is certainly the case. From four-person poker parties to Athena Society events for one hundred guests, the porch is a stylish space in which to congregate, especially when there's a chill in the air and the flickering flames from the fireplace draw everyone near.

Wyldwinde

BARBARA AND BARRY CARROLL — MARTHA'S VINEYARD, MASSACHUSETTS

While the fishermen who built this island community in the nineteenth century have long since passed on, much of New England's glorious maritime history remains afloat in Nantucket Sound. Since Martha's Vineyard is inaccessible by bridge, the view from its bluffs reveals a bounty of island- and mainland-bound vessels below. As crawlers bring lobsters to market, pleasure craft skirt around at a faster clip. Ferries loaded full of "wash-ashore" passengers chug along, while the schooner *Alabama* and square-rigger *Shenandoah* glide by under full sail.

The pageant doesn't stop at the shoreline. From the expansive porch of their 1890s Queen Anne cottage, Barbara and Barry Carroll and their clan of children and grandchildren watch and wave as parents with their tots in strollers, joggers and neighbors walking their dogs pass by. It's a welcoming hostess, this porch, one of the formidable "Gray Ladies" dressed in "skirts of weathered cedar shingles," as Barry describes it. While open to the world, it's also a universe unto itself, with an exposed-beam ceiling above multiple seating areas for the tall and small alike tucked into its curves, including period wicker sets that came with the house. The porch measures twenty feet wide in some places, so it can host lots

LEFT: A line of rockers is ready for watching the passing ships from beneath the shelter of Wyldwinde's exposed-beam ceiling.

OPPOSITE: The Victorian Bar Harbor wicker was included as part of the purchase of the home. The paisley fabric is by Duralee.

of people without ever feeling crowded. "We've had so many gatherings out here, from tea parties to informal island get-togethers, and baby showers to our fortieth anniversary party," Barbara says. Barry adds, "It's wide enough that the grandchildren can race their miniature cars, the sort of space you gravitate toward."

He continues, "The East Chop neighborhood is a cul-de-sac, so it's quieter than our neighbor Oak Bluffs, which is abuzz with traffic from the anchored cruise ships." It's a sort of safe harbor from the storms of tourists who are barhopping just a few miles away. But while it may be quiet here under normal circumstances, "Wyldwinde" has earned its name. "During our first visit, a summer storm came through, and the whole house howled and whistled," Barbara recalls. The family's primary home in the Chicago area is Wyldwoode, so the name for the sister residence came naturally. Winter weather can be alarming: when nor'easters come through, they hit squarely on this northeast corner of the peninsula, and then it's time to run for the shutters and batten down the hatches, although the knowledge that the house has stood for a century brings comfort in even the worst gales.

ABOVE: Barry often greets the day in all its rosy glory. A Pawleys Island hammock is cushioned with a down-filled pillow and a woven throw.

To be sure, inclement weather won't keep the Carrolls at bay; Vineyarders, even part-timers like the Carrolls, are an independent and hardy lot. The island's reputation as a progressive community began with the peaceful coexistence between the English settlers who arrived in the seventeenth century and the Wampanoag tribe (the descendants of whom still live on the island), and continued to be earned in the last century as it became a haven for African-American and Jewish families who were less welcomed at other resort destinations. In 1977 there was a movement afoot for the Vineyard, along with neighboring Nantucket, to secede from the Commonwealth of Massachusetts over issues of insufficient representation. The Carrolls proudly fly the independence flag.

While many island home owners visit mainly during the summer season, Barbara and Barry are frequently in residence, flying back and forth from Illinois on their Mooney 201 plane so that they can enjoy the rosy sunrise from the porch, whether it's surrounded by snow or the blooms of heirloom hydrangeas that ring its railings in the summer.

ABOVE: The Gray Lady Wyldwinde has stood proudly above Nantucket Sound for nearly twelve decades, surviving nor'easters and active grandchildren alike. Heirloom privet hedges rim the porch.

FARM PORCHES

Valley oaks, lindens, deodar cedars and a towering Washingtonia palm
are among the noble trees planted in 1882 by George Schonewald at
this St. Helena, California, estate; the parklike grounds frame what is now
the residence for Mary Novak's award-winning Spottswoode vineyard.

Brown Woods Farm

WILLY BROWN AND EDDIE WOODS — STAMPING GROUND, KENTUCKY

Far off the beaten path from Lexington, Kentucky, Brown Woods Farm is a genuine escape—just as Eddie Woods intended when he purchased the property forty years ago. In 1999, he and his partner, Willy Brown, domesticated the grounds a bit by building a salvaged barn-wood weekend cabin, which, now cloaked in Virginia creeper and trumpet vine, looks as though it has stood for generations.

Behind the cabin lies an expanse of flagstone paving that frames a central fire pit and a spring-fed swimming pond surrounded by pastures dotted with cedar, hickory and oak trees. The landscaped border of native grasses, black-eyed Susans and pear tomatoes nestles up to the fence, as do the Angus-Charolais cattle whose lowing creates a pleasantly bucolic sound track.

Across the patio, a beguiling guest cottage is newly constructed from salvaged glass doors and windows garnered from more than twenty structures. Both the cabin and the cottage include charming porches, but of the two, the latter's is the more unexpected. Beneath the shelter of the corrugated steel roof, mismatched chairs around a picnic table are perfect for having a drink, reading the paper or sampling cheeses from the Trappist Abbey at Gethsemani, all while breathing in the air scented by Eddie's thirty-five varieties of roses.

LEFT: Artist Matt Foley's sculpture *Down* is carved from a section of fused local limestone and sandstone.

OPPOSITE: Hickory logs warm an October twilight in one of three fire pits. The glass guest cottage was created with salvaged materials from more than twenty structures.

ABOVE LEFT: Mismatched chairs add to the atmosphere of "salvage chic." Regional delicacies enjoyed outside include a goat cheese wrapped in grape leaves and raffia from Capriole Farms and a smoked cheese from the Trappist Abbey at Gethsemani.

ABOVE RIGHT: The brass lizard door pulls were a surprise find in a New Orleans junk shop.

RIGHT: Where buffalo once roamed and stamped, now Angus-Charolais cattle graze.

OPPOSITE: A picnic table bar serves as a contemporary drinking hole accented by last-breath-of-summer flowers and a basket of Osage oranges, also known as hedge apples. When placed in the home, the bright green fruit is said to ward off spiders.

A simple gauze curtain shields eyes from the gas grill. With its sliding doors open, the entire cottage feels like a porch, courtesy of all that glass.

Some of the chairs are leave-behinds from clients of Willy's furniture restoration company, Morningside Woodcrafters; others he built using remnants from various projects. "I enjoy using reclaimed materials," Willy explains, "whether they're from friends, or I just buy them off the backs of trucks. It's nice to see the boards and windows get second chances."

The quaint appearance of the cabin and guest cottage can be deceiving. Most of the year, the two structures accommodate perhaps eight close friends. But during the first weekend in October, the pastures and porches become ground zero for a highly anticipated and raucous celebration. Where roaming buffalo herds once found the salt licks and limestone springs on their way through central Kentucky, today visiting hordes of partygoers gather for an entirely more intoxicating form of liquid refreshment.

Many guests stay the night rather than brave dogleg turns in the country roads when only the moon and stars light the way. Hardier revelers claim the sole hammock or toss down a sleeping bag next to one of three fire pits, while others construct refined five-room tents, complete with chandeliers, sterling and crystal. "Our campouts began in the 1980s as a fairly private thing," Willy explains, "but now it's routine for well over one hundred people—only *most* of whom we know—to join us!"

The casual decor of the porches suits the carefree party atmosphere, where one need not worry about putting feet up, crumbs tumbling or wax dripping down onto the tablecloth. While the unspoiled environs, inventive structures and promise of a great party might be what draws friends here, it's the owners' hospitality and humor that make guests reluctant to leave.

LEFT: Virginia creeper and native grasses surround the main cabin, constructed from salvaged barn wood.

A Gardener's Porch

MARY NOVAK — ST. HELENA, CALIFORNIA

When Mary Novak was a child in Los Angeles County, she whiled away the free hours nurturing young plants in a slatted lath house built for her by her father. But being a self-styled country girl, she dreamed of bigger stretches of earth: "I always thought I'd live on a ranch out west someday—it was a *My Friend Flicka* fantasy," she recalls. All of those years working with soil and sprouting seeds paid off handsomely; decades later, she would become not only a farmer, but one of the first female vintners in the country. The literal fruits of her labors have yielded stunning results: wine critic Robert Parker describes the 2005 Cabernet Sauvignon Estate from her Spottswoode vineyard as "utterly profound."

Mary acquired the estate home and vineyard property with her late husband, Jack, in 1972. Architecturally, the focal point of the 46-acre ranch is the Victorian house that sits within the parklike grounds. Built in 1882 by an immigrant hotelier named George Schonewald, the design features a glazed front porch with a gallery of round windows and an unusual wood colonnade inspired by the Hotel Del Monte in Monterey, which Schonewald once managed. When she discovered the house, Mary saw in the old porch a relaxed spot where five children under the age of

LEFT: A collection gathered by Mary on trips across the United States and Europe hints at her self-proclaimed status as a "wise old owl."

OPPOSITE: A combination of metal, wood and wicker furnishings offers an informality to what might otherwise be a formal space, given the noble old architecture.

ABOVE: The view of the glazed porch through the craggy branches of a grand old magnolia shows the colonnade that original owner George Schonewald borrowed from the design of the Hotel Del Monte in Monterey.

LEFT: A service porch off the kitchen features statues of St. Francis from the family's Mexican sojourns.

OPPOSITE: Architectural detailing, including an ornate gallery of round windows, a decorative brass doorknob and wrought-iron railings, is a telltale sign of the house's Victorian heritage.

fifteen could congregate and the family could dine. Decades later, several of her grandchildren live near enough to enjoy the porch.

Although it sees less pitter-patter of little feet these days, the space is comfortably appointed with wicker and metal seating for eight or more. In addition, the front steps are a natural place to sit and peer up into the magnificent limbs and leaves arching overhead, or across to a trickling Mexican stone fountain that catches the light while birds fly past. The landscaping represents a Victorian approach to collecting, which was to include one of everything—and the more rare, the better. Schonewald (the name means "beautiful forest" in German) selected Valley oaks, lindens, deodar cedars, palms and a rare Chinese pagoda tree, among many other varieties, to shade and ornament the grounds. A Washingtonia palm is well over 100 feet tall, making it among the loftiest in Napa Valley.

Having inherited minimal foundation plantings around the porch, Mary put her love of gardening to immediate use in installing camellias and shade-loving hellebores beneath the railings. She also began the watering can collection that now decorates the front porch itself. Her collector's instinct is apparent as well in the gathering of owl statues that she acquired during trips across Europe and the United States. In her words, "At this point in my life, I think I've earned the right to call myself a 'wise old owl'!" She extends her love for these birds to the natural world, too: owl boxes are placed around the farm for nesting.

The service porch attached to the kitchen is a napping room for the family's two black Labs. It also serves as a reminder of the family's former life in Rancho Santa Fe, with the presence of souvenirs from their trips to nearby Mexico including a rustic wood bench and statues of St. Francis. An ornate Victorian wrought-iron railing rims the porch.

St. Helena has become the most fashionable Napa Valley address, with celebrities and financiers purchasing "weekend vineyards" and people from all over touching down for tastings and a peek at the lifestyles of those who are living the dream. None has pursued that dream with more hard work—and success—than Mary Novak. From her lovely front porch at the foot of the Mayacamas mountain range, she can look proudly over all she tends.

RIGHT: Rustic Mexican crosses hang beside an antique grape-harvesting basket, perfect for displaying decorative seasonal trimmings from the gardens like this dogwood branch.

BELOW: Needlepoint pillows stitched by Mary and her mother add a whimsical, colorful touch to the porch's seating.

OPPOSITE: Orange clivia sprays spill from watering cans from Mary's collection. The latticed metal chairs surrounding a glass-topped wicker-based table were purchased in Charleston, South Carolina.

Nursery Place

MARTIE AND JOHN MAYER — CLARK COUNTY, KENTUCKY

Morning and naptime, dinnertime and evening—nearly all year long—Martie and John Mayer live with sons Walker and Griffin and corgis Archi and Ellie Mae on a contemporary screened porch in the Bluegrass State's storied Iroquois Hunt Club region. The site for the soaring structure, the edge of a paddock for thoroughbred brood mares, allows the Mayers to admire and appreciate the surrounding landscape and its heritage, which is so deeply entwined with their own family lineage.

It was to this "promised land" that John Mayer's great-great-grandfather John Fauntleroy Jones traveled the Wilderness Road with his brother Thomas Ap Jones in the 1780s. Aspiring nurserymen, the pair brought linden and bald cypress saplings to establish a 5,000-acre farm that became the foundation for orchards and nurseries across the territory, which was then still a part of Virginia. The Jones brothers built a brick homestead, which remains on the Mayers' 350-acre farm; Martie and John's house was constructed more than two hundred years later just

LEFT: An antique wooden mixing bowl with Honeycrisps and Granny Smiths rests on a split hickory bench that serves as a coffee table.

OPPOSITE: The tree-trunk side table was made by John from a felled maple on the property. Oriole, pheasant, mockingbird, red-tailed hawk and wild turkey feathers collected during family walks on the property sit in a presidential mint julep cup given to Walker Haggin Mayer, John and Martie's son, by his godfather.

up the hill along the historic Jones Nursery Road, which was the route for taking fruit and trees to market.

The area's history doesn't run only in John's blood, though; Martie's family has been a significant force in the equine industry. Her great-grandfather Hal Price Headley was cofounder of Keeneland, Lexington's esteemed racetrack. Hal's daughter was Martie's grandmother Alma Haggin, who was instrumental in the landscaping and interior design of the gracious Keeneland clubhouse. Meanwhile, her grandfather Louis Lee Haggin was president of the track for a decade. "John's and my grandparents

ABOVE: The red lacquer frames of split hickory chairs were washed with a walnut stain to create a warmer tone. In the background, Emmaus, a fifteen-year-old stakes-winning chestnut brood mare, enjoys a feeding in a split-rail paddock.

were friends," Martie notes, "which makes the story of our meeting and becoming a family even more special to us."

Martie clearly inherited her grandmother's talent for interior design, but John was also an active force in the styling of the two-story porch. Although the modern beamed space might have proved difficult to make cozy given its dimensions, the knotty pine ceiling, pine floors stained a shade of butterscotch, and walnut-washed red lacquer accents confer warmth. Also welcoming is the mix of comfortable furnishings that the couple collected with year-round use in mind. All-weather wicker, fade- and water-resistant Scalamandré fabric and both hickory and wrought-iron tables and chairs withstand sun, wind and rain for use at all times of day, in every season. (And, they tolerate wear and tear from two teenage sons.)

In more protected areas, split hickory chairs and benches add texture and regional charm. Concealed lights run along the ceiling's edge to provide gentle uplighting of the architecture, while antler lighting fixtures from Highlands, North Carolina, add a rustic presence. The swinging custom daybed was modeled after one the couple enjoyed while visiting the Greyfield Inn on Cumberland Island, off the coast of Georgia. One very special table was hewn from a maple tree felled on the property. John cut, buffed, stained and painted a section of the trunk for a small chairside table next to where he reads his Bible at dawn, with a chorus of waking robins, goldfinches and cardinals to accompany him. "Even in the winter I'll be out here—the only difference is I might be wearing a parka!" he says.

ABOVE: Ellie Mae runs by a birdhouse designed by Larry Smith of It's for the Birds. The design is based on the Clarkesville [Georgia] Grace Episcopal Church designed by Savannah architect Robert Dowling.

RIGHT: With proportions drawn from a similar model found on Cumberland Island, this swinging daybed lures the weary to nap and the slightly more industrious to hook a rug or read.

Kortum Canyon Porches

MARY AND ROB MORROW — CALISTOGA, CALIFORNIA

"I'm not impressed by 'important' antiques just because they're valuable, and I won't be pressured to display them if they don't suit my own or my client's style," designer Mary Morrow declares. Describing her approach to interiors as "biographical design," Mary believes that souvenirs, photographs, diplomas and family heirlooms should be integrated into the decor of the home to build each room's story. She and her husband, Rob, have known each other since the second grade, so there's no shortage of shared memories in their cozy Napa Valley weekend retreat.

The three-bedroom home is a raised cottage, a vernacular style most commonly found along the Gulf Coast. The breeze-friendly position above the seasonally flooded or rain-soaked earth, tall ceilings that held heat away from those sitting or sleeping and wrapping porches that kept the sun and rains at bay were all vital architectural details in the South. While flooding is not a major concern in Kortum Canyon, it can get very hot in the summer, so the lofty ceilings and shady porches offer welcome relief. The home served as the centerpiece of the 284-acre Dietz Ranch, an orchard for walnuts and plums that began as a Spanish land grant.

LEFT: The view past ancient Douglas firs into Kortum Canyon is breathtaking at all times of the day, and throughout the year.

OPPOSITE: A patchwork throw crocheted by Mary's mother helps to build a snuggly nest on a Pawleys Island hammock that was given to Mary and Rob as a wedding present. Coffee-bean sacks serve as informal area rugs.

LEFT: Tall windows and wrapping porches are key features of raised cottages, intended to aid in cooling homes such as these that are more commonly found along the hot and humid Gulf Coast. A substantial chipped-paint worktable is filled with the makings of a feast. Firecrackers and lanterns purchased when the family lived in Hong Kong build a sense of festive excitement.

BELOW: The farmhouse was the primary residence for the Dietz Ranch, which produced prunes and walnuts. The walnuts are displayed in an antique Chinese water scoop.

OPPOSITE: On the back porch, croquet mallets, badminton racquets and a baseball glove illustrate the family's active lifestyle and sense of fun.

The property was divided in the 1970s, but the view from the porches at this 850-foot elevation remains pristine. With stunning vistas of the upper Napa Valley glimpsed through towering 300-year-old Douglas firs, the home is enveloped by a seemingly endless sea of rolling blue-green hills.

While the six-foot-wide porch decking doesn't allow for facing chairs, Mary enjoys both quiet solitude and intimate tête-à-têtes from sunrise to dusk and beyond. "The porch is just a different zone, a sort of bridge space. I'm not sure if it's because we're looking out in one direction and so are not scrutinizing each other as we speak, but we all seem to open up differently out there."

Mary's ironclad rules about personal history and decor apply on her two porches, one that hugs the house on three sides and the other at a rear entrance. A Pawleys Island hammock that was a wedding gift to the couple is hung at one corner of the larger porch, overlooking a "spiritual vortex" grove of fir trees that landscape designer and energy diviner Roger Warner credits with having a high frequency of creative energy. Cushioning the hammock is a colorful patchwork throw crocheted by Mary's mother from snippets of yarn; underfoot are burlap coffee-bean sacks from a local coffee shop, which serve as casual area rugs.

Raised in New Orleans, Mary fell in love with the farmhouse at first sight, taken in by its similarities to houses prevalent in her delta hometown. This getaway exudes Southern hospitality in its comfort and sense of welcome. But, while it hosts local vintners sharing wines at neighborhood parties, the porch is primarily a family sanctuary. Following their annual Christmas Eve hike into Kortum Canyon to see the Palisades and Mount St. Helena, an alfresco luncheon of Southern favorites—including ham, corn bread and red beans and rice—is served. The food, the view and the belongings are all in harmony. As Mary defines it, "Creating traditions and sticking to them builds memories, which in turn makes us feel held in this house; it embraces us with all its history."

A Vineyard Porch

VIRGINIA AND ERNEST VAN ASPEREN — ST. HELENA, CALIFORNIA

Nearly four decades ago, Ernest Van Asperen traded in his career in restaurants and liquor stores for a chance at winemaking. He bought a Napa Valley hilltop with his wife, Virginia, and before long friends were helping to pick, stomp, bottle and hand-label small batches at the Van Asperens' home. As their knowledge and success increased, they purchased a pre-Prohibition facility (known in the trade as a ghost winery) to formalize the process. When the couple finally decided to sell that operation, they were producing 400,000 cases a year of Round Hill varieties including cabernet sauvignon, chardonnay and sauvignon blanc.

The nerve center and social nexus of the enterprise was the couple's contemporary ranch-style home. While Virginia was not originally stirred by the 1955 structure—it was the enviable acreage she and her husband had fallen for—she has come to "respect, and even adore" the solid construction and ease of single-floor living. Once the Van Asperens retired, the view down the valley became much less about what

LEFT: The lights come up as the sun sets on Napa Valley.

OPPOSITE: The seating was custom-designed by Erin Martin and locally constructed from redwood planks. The silk-screened pillows are by Mia Rela; the cushions are covered with a Sunbrella all-season canvas. Virginia hand-carried the collection of ostrich eggs from Oudtshoorn, South Africa; the small round sculpture of canvas strips is by her friend (and fellow vintner) Eli Coppola.

LEFT: Japanese maples are anchored in sturdy cement planters. A trio of antique Thai pier pulls adds exotic texture to the clean lines of the porch.

BELOW: Ivory benches are topped with photographic Cow Skull and Zinnia pillows by Archival Decor. The Pol's Potten porcelain detergent bottles are from Martin Showroom.

must be done for and to the grapes to fool Mother Nature, and more about enjoying the beauty the vine-striped hills offer. They are picturesque through the four seasons; large glass windows bring the view right into the living room. "I always look forward to the beauty here as I drive up the twisting roads," Virginia admits. "It's like a resort."

In retirement, the couple scaled back their entertaining in favor of smaller gatherings, so nationally recognized (but locally based) interiors and furniture designer Erin Martin helped to transform their porch accordingly. The space has become both restful and intimate, truly extending the living area of the house. "I asked Erin for an overscale look with comfortable, stationary furnishings that could remain outside throughout the year," Virginia says.

The elements of the porch are as balanced and easy to enjoy as a smooth chardonnay, and none requires cautious handling. The space is enhanced underfoot by the rosy Mexican tile floor and overhead with soothing and unifying ivory plank eaves. A former sculptor, Martin anchored the seating area with a custom-made love seat and club chairs designed with redwood planks and fitted with deep cushions that she covered in outdoor fabric. The rest of the porch is easily cared for, too, including the square concrete coffee table designed by Martin. "Lots of birds nest in the eaves, so it's important that the table can be hosed off," Virginia explains. Side tables and the substantial pots for two Japanese maple trees are also of concrete. The dining table outside the kitchen seats six for casual

suppers, with the Van Asperens' best vintages complementing dolmas made with grape leaves fresh off the vine. Above it all, a sixteen-light wrought-iron chandelier crowns the open, airy space, its rusted finish of a piece with the colors of the stained-wood furniture. Virginia recounts: "In the late seventies, a farmer pulled his truck in front of our offices and asked, 'Does anyone want a chandelier?' and I instantly said, 'I'll take it!'"

Two guest rooms open directly onto the porch rather than into the house, thus giving privacy and easy access to the pool and gardens. A single slatted teak table and chair just outside those rooms offer a meditative spot with a view of the vineyards; three antique Thai pier pulls stand as serene, and unexpected, sculptures. "Erin asked me to trust her when the design process began," Virginia explains, "and I could not be happier with the results."

ABOVE: The view of the early spring vineyards at twilight only hints at the bounty to come. Ceramic bisque campfire logs by KleinReid rest on a teak table.

Orchard Porches

KAREN AND TIM BATES — PHILO, CALIFORNIA

Given the necessities of farm life—from managing the land, crops and livestock to keeping equipment and buildings in good repair—it is a rare breed of family who find the inspiration, much less the time, to add the handcrafting of design elements into their daily routines.

Karen and Tim Bates, along with their four children, are just such people. Karen describes the efforts for their 1,600-tree Philo Apple Farm (and cooking school, with guest cottages) as a matter of balance—between priorities and pleasures, between earning a living and feeding the senses and the soul. From an aesthetic point of view, she says "it's about knowing when things are out of balance, and working as an editor to correct colors, textures, forms and moods."

Karen cultivated this talent for editing over a lifetime of experience. After painting and sewing in her early years, she later designed clothing and assisted with The French Laundry, the iconic Napa Valley restaurant—hailed as one of the finest in the country—which her parents, Sally and Don Schmitt, established and operated for many years. "You learn to get rid of what isn't important, and emphasize what is—and then try to carry that lesson into the other spheres of your life," she observes.

LEFT: A lamp shade made by Karen from pierced sandalwood fan blades casts an inviting glow in the evening.

OPPOSITE: A potter's wheel on daughter Rita's porch is but one of many indications of artists at work on the farm. Metal barrel hoops rest beneath the skylight.

The balance between living indoors and out brings harmony to daily life on the farm. While the Bateses spend the bulk of their waking hours in the fresh air, they also prefer to be outside when they're "off duty," and the northern California climate permits this through most of the year. Their houses, cabins and even gypsy caravans all include porches and decks; they built most with their own hands in collaboration with various craftsmen. "Our goal for all of the structures was to be light on the land—to use as little material as possible, as well as those that are least harmful, and to have lots of air and sunlight throughout all. The porches in particular are incredibly valuable to us."

The main residence was built using ancient rammed-earth construction (also known as *pisé de terre:* a wooden frame is filled with packed dirt mixed with hay, sand, gravel, clay and other elements, all stabilized with cement), while the guest cottages are formed from galvanized steel and pressure-treated Douglas fir. The cottages are arranged in a conversation with one another— close enough to call out to a neighboring porch sitter, but with enough distance between them to ensure privacy. Furnished with a variety of vintage chairs and benches, the exterior living spaces are spare but inviting. "We use what we have; our financial priorities are always farm related, not decor related, so our design solutions have to come from what's on hand," Karen explains. The textures of the steel and wood beams add a level of depth to the simple A-frame silhouettes, while pillows and plants soften the modern look. Solar lighting fixtures, attached near the steps rather than the walls, help guide guests' feet on the stairs through starry nights.

Additional outdoor living areas include an arbor of entwined mulberry tree branches, which is reminiscent of a vaulted church ceiling, and a dining space featuring a Moroccan tile table and decorative steel fire pit designed by Stevan Derwinski, which lies between the arbor and the farm's cooking school cabin. On the latter's porch, wooden stools serve as occasional tables beside simple metal chairs, and a rope "chain" hangs in the rainspout, allowing downpours to flow over its braid into a rain barrel. A shallow overhang keeps heat out and rain off the doors without blocking the view from the dining table inside.

The back deck of the main house faces the orchard. A mattress and throw pillows cover a vintage painted cast-iron bed that serves as a favorite Sunday resting spot for Karen. A woven window shade draped over an iron-frame open "house" provides cover once the grapevines that climb its rails fill in each spring. The coming and going of winged friends, the blossoming apple trees and the Mendocino County hills are among the many natural wonders seen from this vantage point. While the funky resort ambience and "cool factor" might be deceptive, the calls of goats, pigs, horses and mules are a constant reminder that this is a working farm.

Karen and her daughter, Rita, worked for two weeks building a pair of whimsical gypsy wagons as an experiment in creating alternative (and movable) housing for guests. Under the guidance of a Canadian craftswoman, they designed and hand-constructed these miniature rooms, which offer a delightful splash of color and unexpected shape on the orchard's grounds. Both wagons have steel roofs and small front porches just big enough for visitors to sit on and dangle their feet over.

BELOW: Colorful gypsy wagons on the property were hand-built by Karen and her daughter, Rita. With double beds, built-in bookshelves and small front porches, they're worlds unto themselves.

OPPOSITE: A handwritten message on a chalkboard invites people to explore, but asks that they be courteous while doing so. The Bateses' apples are known as Philo Golds; artist Laura Parker created this painting (center) for the produce porch to honor the stars of the orchard's show. Chutney, jam, balsamic vinegar (below), hard cider and syrup are all for sale.

ABOVE: The circular lawn in front of the cooking school cabin is the only manicured area of the property; the children used it for their acrobatic play while the dogs ran the circle like a tiny racetrack around them. The Moroccan tile table is from Furnishings for Friends, a collection established by Karen's sister-in-law, Melissa Schmitt. An applewood fire warms a cool spring evening in a steel fire pit designed by Stevan Derwinski.

RIGHT: A copper and steel sideboard also designed by Derwinski echoes the entwined branches overhead.

LEFT: To form this vaulted arbor, mulberry tree whips (young branchless saplings) required gardening processes called pollarding and pleaching (as well as constant pruning). Round bulbs strung across it create a magical environment for dining and dancing.

Even the farm's produce stand is a porch of sorts. Wooden shelves are filled with luscious chutneys, apple balsamic vinegar, hard cider and jams. A painting of their Philo Gold apples by Laura Parker hangs behind the glowing colors of the display.

All of these elements combine to create an environment that offers the Bates family ample opportunity to appreciate their labors and enjoy their well-earned rests. Beauty lies everywhere, from cider-barrel-hoop sculptures made by Karen, which serve to protect young plants from curious beaks, to thriving flowering bushes and original furniture designed by son Joe and local craftsmen.

Throughout the farm, the contemporary and the traditional work hand in hand, from farm methods to architecture and furnishings. The Bates residence is an original vision that is wholly at home in this Anderson Valley orchard.

BELOW: Midcentury butterfly chairs invite guests to "sit a spell" and share the beauty of the orchard.

OPPOSITE: A house-shaped frame on the deck behind the main residence fills out with trellised grapevines, creating a "roof" that provides shade for the napping bed (earlier in the season, a woven window shade suffices).

Woodland Farm

LAURA LEE BROWN AND STEVE WILSON — GOSHEN, KENTUCKY

A collection of artful surprises greets visitors to the nineteenth-century brick farmhouse that stands proudly on the rolling hills of Woodland Farm. The fields were essentially fallow when Laura Lee Brown and Steve Wilson purchased the property in the 1990s, but the couple envisioned the restoration of the house and its lands to working farmland "as a win-win situation for us and for the community," Steve says. To start their Kentucky Bison Company here, they acquired twenty-five buffalo calves from Custer State Park in South Dakota. "We grew up on farms and had a desire to return to that life we both remember so fondly," he explains.

As the masterminds behind Louisville's dynamic 21c Museum Hotel concept, these committed contemporary art collectors have cleverly blended the natural and historic with works by notable modern artists in their home. Just beyond their side porch, near the edge of a spring-fed pond, stands a life-sized bronze equine sculpture by artist Deborah Butterfield, while herds of buffalo peaceably add their own brand of ambience, like pioneer-themed *tableaux vivants,* in the adjoining fields. In the process of restoring the homestead, the couple introduced the unpretentious porch. Spending much of the workweek in the city, they wanted to enjoy

LEFT: Traditional peg and board and dry-stack stone were among the building methods used to construct the new porch.

OPPOSITE: Noted contemporary art collectors Laura Lee and Steve punctuate their nineteenth-century farm with new works such as this armchair designed from local driftwood by Eric Scholtens.

LEFT: The porch, with its view of the Ohio River, is the perfect breakfast nook. The arrow-back chairs are from a local antique shop. The cast-bronze sculpture is by Larry Shank.

BELOW: Laura Lee's great-grandfather George Garvin Brown was the founder of the family's spirits empire, which today includes Jack Daniel's and Finlandia. His handwriting, as seen on bottles of Old Forester, decorates a limited-edition set of china made for the Brown family.

OPPOSITE: On close summer nights, the reproduction belt-and-pulley ceiling fans offer relief. In cooler weather, a satin-lined fox lap rug on the teak swing provides a luxe nest for the couple (and assorted pets).

their land and the view of the Ohio River from the bluff on which the house sits while having breakfast. Their commitment to history is apparent in the measures taken to attach the porch seamlessly to the old house, under the tutelage of noted Virginia-based preservationist William Seale, who has guided the restorations of numerous state capitols and other historic buildings nationwide.

The porch sits atop a mortarless dry-stack stone foundation—a regional feature introduced by Scotch-Irish immigrants—and its roofing is of recycled lumber from an abandoned chicken coop. Pegged floorboards add another level of historic immersion with their absence of nails, while antique arrow-back chairs, a battered farmhouse table, and belt-and-pulley ceiling fans further contribute to the nineteenth-century mood. A high-backed chair newly crafted by Eric Scholtens from armloads of local driftwood is a refreshingly contemporary, but fitting, addition to the environment, while a cast-bronze sculpture by Larry Shank of a pair of rabbits sawing away at a loaf of bread adds a touch of humor.

Between the porch and the river lies a terrace of Lee sandstone quarried on the southern side of the state, in McCreary County. Landscape architect Mac Reid's plans for the property included the introduction of native trees such as beech and crab apple, and also the Shumard oaks that line both sides of the drive in ascending height, forming an allée. "They connect to the residence, as if the oaks are pulling you toward it magnetically," he says.

On rainy days, the eight-mile-long view from the porch across the river reveals trees in Indiana, fading in and out of drifting fog banks. Barges laden with goods cautiously ply those same waters, while closer by raindrops cast interlocking ripples onto the surface of the pond. The home's protected site on the bluffs is close enough to civilization to be private but not isolated; Louisville is less than an hour away.

Mist and rain bring precious moisture to the fenced dooryard garden behind the house, which was designed in part by Mac's wife, Tay Breene. This flower and herb garden harkens back to the period when roaming creatures were fenced out rather than in. "The sense of enormity of Woodland Farm is unique in Kentucky, which is generally more enclosed and intimate," Mac notes. "It's akin to the big sky feeling in the West."

ABOVE: A historic marker tells the story of the farm's origins and the buffalo enterprise that Laura Lee and Steve introduced in an effort to return the land to its origins.

OPPOSITE: Ripples reach for shore on the spring-fed pond located a stone's throw from the porch. The bronze sculptures are by Marvin Hirn.

URBAN PORCHES

At the Lexington, Kentucky, home of Becky and Reese Reinhold, skylights offer additional illumination to a second-floor rear porch. A painting by local artist Carolyn Young Hisel hangs above the brick fireplace. The metal-frame furniture is by Summer Classics; the pillows by Dwell are from Mulberry & Lime; the ceramic tile floor is by Impronta Ceramiche Italgraniti.

The Professional Porch Sitters Union

CLAUDE AND ERIN STEPHENS — LOUISVILLE, KENTUCKY

By day, Claude Stephens is the mild-mannered education director for Bernheim Arboretum and Research Forest in Clermont, Kentucky. On nights and weekends, back home in his Irish Hills neighborhood in Louisville, however, he transforms into a charismatic social revolutionary and community superhero.

For more than two hundred years, the Stephens family have been perfecting wonderfully imperfect Louisville porches that are completely free from pretense and are filled with personal touches, including handmade quilts and benches made from the flatboats that carried their family's belongings down the Ohio River from Lancaster County, Pennsylvania. Claude founded the Professional Porch Sitters Union (Local 1339, as it's known to Union members) one meeting-weary day in 1999 as he was decompressing with friends on his double-shotgun home's clapboard and concrete porch. After indulging in a Louisville-appropriate

LEFT: Claude created a series of thirteen dolls from household trash. This one, called *Ouch*, includes a cardboard incense container, a Band-Aid box, Yoo-Hoo bottle caps and a Fritos bag. He also painted a series of torsos, including *Nurse Man*, shown here.

OPPOSITE: Claude chose his porch name, Crow, to honor his grandfather, who promised he'd become one of the wise black birds after passing away and would watch out for the boy in that form. Claude has collected the birds ever since; they're joined by midcentury dinette chairs, original works of art and a host of vintage shop finds.

beverage (i.e., bourbon), the group began to feel they had accomplished more by shooting the breeze than they had during all of their respective meetings, and an institution was born.

When members are in the neighborhood, Claude and his wife, Erin, hope they'll come and visit. Their sage-green-sided, eggplant-floored space is a friendly, low-maintenance canvas for a host of colorful characters, plants and collections. From stuffed crows to dolls made from trash and from oil paintings to an assemblage of rusty oil cans, it's equal parts gallery, vintage shop and living room. There's a chipped-patina glider just begging for weary bones to rest, and midcentury dinette chairs pulled up to an old farm table offer a couple more spots. If all those seats are taken, visitors can push aside a potted plant and sit on the low and wide concrete railings.

Claude took his instinct for environmental sustainability—honed at the arboretum—and parlayed it into this bid for social sustainability on the home front. As his porch alter ego, Crow Hollister (a name chosen, in part, in honor of the bootlegger on *The Andy Griffith Show*), he wants people to step back from their workplace personas and step into the outdoors among their neighbors. The Union is an informal gathering; if you want to be a member, then *bingo!* count yourself in—all are welcome. Claude talks about how, before air-conditioning, porches served as a place to escape the heat of the kitchen. Families entertained themselves by telling stories (before television), making music (before radio) or playing cards (before video games). They were participants in the creation of their amusements, not just recipients of what others delivered.

Today, sitting in sight of your neighbors may be a small act, but Claude argues that porches remain a low-key venue for tackling the getting-to-know-you's. They're well suited for "being social, but just a step shy of the inner sanctum, which might be less comfortable to open up to people you don't know all that well—yet."

ABOVE: Claude's prize crow admires a shiny bauble from his paperweight collection.

LEFT: An image of Che Guevara below a fragment of the Constitution's text proves a perfect union.

As Union boss, Claude doesn't preach rights and responsibilities, but the simple courage to become active in the community by merely sitting. There are tangible benefits: "Neighborhoods where people know one another are safer, more pleasant places to live," he says. A few casual conversations can convert neighbors who haven't a clue when something goes awry into those who can be counted on during an emergency, or just for that cup of sugar.

Though originally meant in jest, the fledgling Union has been featured on National Public Radio and CBS News. It has inspired like-minded groups throughout the country and abroad (Louisville City Councilman Tom Owen's founding of Front Porch Tuesdays to encourage community involvement surely has echoes of PPSU 1339). Still, of all the contributions that Claude and Erin have made to their own community, none is more tangible than this: a few years after being introduced on this very porch, the couple celebrated the birth of their daughter, Ruby, who is now a proud porch partisan in her own right.

RIGHT: Claude can still describe the fabric pattern on the quilt he wrapped around himself as a child on his family's porch. On his own porch, a quilt from a tall stack of vintage finds offers similar comfort. His collection of rusty oil cans began as a joke—but has grown to include 145 pieces.

A Parkside Retreat

KELLEY AND GREG PARKER — SAVANNAH, GEORGIA

Possessing a wealth of old-growth trees, a grand fountain and an expansive green lawn, Savannah's historic Forsyth Park attracts a flurry of visitors, from joggers and tennis players to picnickers and concertgoers. The gracious view and easy proximity for exercise and dog walking make it an ideal urban "front yard" for those fortunate enough to live along it. But, as some home owners can attest, this popularity can have its downsides, too. "People come right up onto the front porch and look through our windows!" Kelley Parker exclaims. While she understands their fascination with the handsome Italianate house she shares with her husband, Greg, and their three children, it can also be a bit unsettling to see strangers peering inside.

The couple's solution: a louvered privacy screen between their front and side porches to create what is now a well-used, well-loved three-walled room. Now, wandering eyes aren't privy to the family's private outdoor life, whether it's the children at their

LEFT: The landscaped courtyard is a pocket of calm between the house and the busy street just beyond the gate; along with the front and side porches, it offers ample room for seasonal entertaining.

OPPOSITE: Caned mahogany and wicker seating create a comfortable and child- and pet-friendly room for relaxation and dining—one that remains private courtesy of the louvered screen seen at back. The gas lamp is from Circa Lighting. The antique leather medicine balls are from The Paris Market. The framed photograph is by Meryl Truett.

LEFT: Lagustrum topiaries flank the louvered privacy screen's door.

OPPOSITE, ABOVE: The salvaged Deco metal columns incorporated into the courtyard below the porch serve as trellises for climbing ivy.

OPPOSITE, CENTER: The original stucco façade was restored by water-blasting decades of paint away; the resulting texture and variety of tones warm the porch and help to historically anchor the home.

OPPOSITE, BELOW: Kelley and Greg found a pair of stone fountains in Provence; one features the head of Bacchus while the other, pictured here, is that of a lion—an homage to the house's previous life as the Lion's Head Inn.

homework, guests sipping cocktails or Kelley and Greg sharing a quiet moment together after tucking the kids into bed.

Post-restoration, the house is a far cry from the building the couple purchased; architect Randolph Martz colorfully describes its "before" state as akin to a "dark, dank labyrinth from which a minotaur might leap out and attack at any moment." The original glory of the house, which was built in 1883 by William H. Wade and John R. Hamlet, had been diminished by crowding eleven

bedrooms into the layout in order to convert the home into the Lion's Head Inn. It's a fate that befell many of Savannah's historic homes, and one that Kelley and Greg, with their commitment to the restoration of the city's historic district, were eager to help reverse. The original turned-wood Ionic columns on the side porch had been replaced with wrought-iron versions in the 1930s. "Not only was the look historically inappropriate, but the transparent and ephemeral appearance of the columns was too insubstantial beneath the heavy porch entablature," says Randolph. Fortunately, Kelley discovered an old photograph that revealed the home's original columns; these and many other elements were then returned to their nineteenth-century splendor.

Working with their own building company, Parker Construction, the couple water-blasted the original stucco exterior to remove old paint, then "scumbled" the surface tone by lightly applying an opaque film of color to variegate the surface. The scoring of the stucco gives the appearance of substantial stone blocks. "We wanted that charming imperfection that you see on the ancient European stucco façades," says Greg. A vintage chipped-paint wicker daybed, cushioned with a striped canvas-covered mattress and pillows that are pet- and child-proof, is the wall's perfect textural partner. "It's nice to be able to tuck your feet up and not worry about the fabric," says Kelley.

Deeper than most side porches, the space accommodates a caned mahogany settee and chairs gathered around a marble-topped baker's table that can seat the whole family for casual suppers. Antique filigree wrought-iron planters filled with vibrant geraniums and a kumquat tree welcome the morning sun. "The gentle light of an eastern exposure is great for younger and more fragile plants—they don't get scorched," explains Kelley. Floor-to-ceiling windows between the porch and the living room allow an indoor view of this piquant setting.

Between the porch and another grand house next door is a well-manicured courtyard, where decorative and shady trees, climbing plants and a pair of stone fountains create a quiet refuge mere feet from street traffic. The convenience of an urban dwelling, paired with the peace and greenery of a secluded retreat, makes the Parkers' home the very best of both worlds.

Rockhouse

TAMARA AND MAX STRANG — COCONUT GROVE, FLORIDA

Architect Max Strang was magnetically drawn to the tropical—yet civilized and funky—paradise that is Coconut Grove; presumably, that same impulse attracted famous Grove residents over the years like Tennessee Williams, Joni Mitchell and Jimmy Buffett. Amid palm fronds and mammoth leaves in this steamy, upscale Miami enclave, Max's distinctive family home sits harmoniously in its lush surroundings, an example of the "environmental modernism" that his firm practices. The idea was to evoke a rustic Balinese resort, he says, or a game lodge in Zimbabwe. "I think a trip when I was eight to the ruins of the Yucatán peninsula also helped," adds the well-traveled designer, whose friends have described the architecture as "neo-Mayan."

The land was originally home to a 1920s board-and-batten shack on an acre lot that Max occupied for years while design ideas matured in his imagination. First on the agenda was a new rock wall to define the perimeter of the property. Then the architect and his wife, Tamara, rid the overgrown lot of many invasive plant species in order to give the fine old specimens breathing room.

LEFT: Leather-fringed pillows from Mali add color and texture to the neutrally toned porch.

OPPOSITE: Max and Tamara's 2002 trip to Bali, with its shopping excursions to Denpasar and Ubud, yielded a shipping container's worth of unfinished teak and other rustic furniture, which they used to create intimate spaces within the massive span of the porch.

Plenty of mango and papaya trees remain alongside a massive banyan, a baobab tree and live oaks. Add in the requisite palms—fishtail, royal, sable and coconut—and the verdant canopy easily maintains the density to shelter the property from the Florida sun while providing a habitat for mynah birds and lizards. The tropical mood is only heightened when flocks of blue-and-gold macaws alight. (Local lore has it that a breeding pair escaped from the zoo during the aftermath of Hurricane Andrew and began multiplying.)

The clearing on the land called for a slender house that is 155 feet long but just 24 feet wide. Max chose rustic but durable building materials to imply that the structure had stood for generations, and to ensure its survival for many more. For the first-floor walls, he quarried oolitic limestone right on site, from beneath where the house would stand. "You can't get more local than what was underneath the grass," says Max, who had a keen interest in using as much indigenous Florida material as was feasible and aesthetically pleasing. He has been tempted, he says, to allow small trees and climbing vines to root in the walls, a

ABOVE LEFT: Tamara and Max paired a twelve-person teak dining table that was custom-made at the Sriwijaya Workshop in Bali with rustic log benches.

ABOVE RIGHT: A tall teak chest offers storage space and a point of textural interest. The ivory board-and-batten wall is an homage to the 1920s cottage that had stood on the property.

OPPOSITE: More than just creating a beautiful and interesting home, the literally rock-solid construction means that when hurricanes come through, the building doesn't sway a centimeter.

sort of nod to Angkor Wat, but acknowledges "that would wreak havoc" structurally.

The entire second floor is an outdoor deck sheltered under a roof upheld by sixty 36-foot steel beams that appear rusted, thanks to a special iron paint that produces a texture and color suitable to the jungle geography. The resulting effect is a strong visual pairing with the rough-hewn rock. Running the full length of the house, this porch is almost entirely open. Imported Brazilian ipe for the deck easily withstands South Florida's torrential storms and bleaching sun. Without any of the artificial preservatives of other decking, this wood naturally shrugs off both rot and bugs. Ipe also resists splintering—an important feature for the family's barefoot lifestyle.

In such easy and expansive surroundings, crowds are no big deal. The deck wraps an indoor pod with a full kitchen (and a dumbwaiter connected to the main kitchen below), so the Strangs have hosted as many as one hundred for sit-down dinners. Regular gatherings have friends and neighbors sharing mango

favorites—from margaritas to tarts, sherbet served in orange halves and snapper baked with mango in banana leaves—all featuring fruit plucked from nearby trees. As the adults enjoy one another's company, their children are kept in sight (but just out of earshot) in a 150-square-foot entertainment area within the enclosure, which also has a guest bathroom.

Max clad the pods with board-and-batten siding in an homage to the structure he tore down. The surrounding space, with its new stone and steel, could have been quite masculine. Instead, it has a grace that feels peaceful. Rockhouse "has a peculiar way of being bold and sensitive at the same time," he acknowledges. Add the landscaping and warmth of the Balinese wood furnishings, and you're transported to an exotic tropical world—one, in fact, that the house portrayed in the 2006 movie *Miami Vice*, where it served as a drug kingpin's hideaway. "On a good day," Max jokes, "you can see the equator."

Harmony Hill

BEA BOWLES — SAN FRANCISCO, CALIFORNIA

The eighty-two steps to Bea Bowles's front porch might seem daunting, but the journey and the destination are well worth the effort: for each step toward her Craftsman cottage, the fragrant woodland garden provides lush sights and scents (and an excuse to stop and catch one's breath), and once the summit is reached, the expansive views offer a great reward. "When people finally make it to the top, they're exhausted and ecstatic at the same time!" Bea exclaims.

The hallmarks of an Arts and Crafts house—the handcrafting, the clean lines, the warm materials, the honoring of nature—are all represented in this home. Designed by architect Albert Farr and constructed entirely from California redwood, it was notched into Russian Hill in 1906 on four levels and features seven porches facing each direction, or "eyes on all sides," as Bea describes them. The house is the perfect perch for watching the ships in the bay and enjoying the sparkling lights of the Transamerica Pyramid and Grace Cathedral.

The welcome on the front porch begins with a cheerful red lacquer door and McGuire chairs surrounded by ceramic planters

LEFT: Grace Cathedral is but one of many famous San Francisco landmarks that can be seen from Harmony Hill.

OPPOSITE: A framed section of Chinese wallpaper adds sunshiny warmth to the front porch while a garden stool and planter amplify the Asian motif. The Transamerica Pyramid is reflected in the glass.

LEFT: The red lacquer door adds a lively splash of color to this redwood-shingled Craftsman cottage; red McGuire chairs extend its cheer. With 90 panes of glass, the foyer remains light-filled through most of the day.

BELOW: A stack of antiquarian gardening editions topped by pewter-dipped branches mixes period-appropriate and modern ornamental accents.

overflowing with petunias, rhododendrons and aromatic rosemary. The red entry sparks up the brown-shingled exterior, and
Asian motifs found in the oversized pair of framed hand-painted
Chinese wallpaper sections and ceramic garden stools add an
exotic touch appropriate for this Pacific Rim city. Ninety panes of
glass in eighteen windows allow the sunshine to stream into the
house. A brass claddagh door knocker honors Bea's Irish heritage;
flanking the doors, a pair of bronze Buddhist hands holding lotus

ABOVE: A cozy pergola was added to the
back of the house to create an intimate dining
space beneath the terraced gardens. A pair
of majolica parrots and a planter handmade
by a group of schoolchildren in thanks for
one of Bea's storytelling sessions add rich
color and sheen to the table.

flowers expresses her beliefs about the vital presence of loving-kindness in the world.

At the back of the house, Bea added a cozy pergola to create an intimate space from what had been an open terrace. A set of redwood chairs and tables with relief carvings of woodland creatures from the Filoli Estate provide ample low-maintenance seating while antique Chinese bamboo garden chairs with ink-wash illustrations serve as stylish and comfortable counterpoints. Bea arranged statues of Quan Yin, the goddess of mercy, in a shrine along one wall and at the far end of the open space. In the evenings, when she entertains her friends or simply enjoys an alfresco supper alone, colorful glass candleholders hanging from the shrubs and trees create a romantic space. A rare cork oak planted by her grandmother towers above the terraced garden; the whole environment evokes childhood memories of her family's living on this hill, which at the turn of the last century was populated by artists and spiritualists. "It was a wild bohemian land in those days," she recalls. "As children, we used to run around like untamed creatures."

With the constant presence of doves, finches and emerald green parrots, this veritable aviary helps continue that wild spirit. When the fog rolls and creeps from the ocean down the hill toward the bay, enveloping the house and trees in its thick silver cloud, a layer of mystery cloaks the home, too. With secret stepping-stone pathways leading into thickets, flocks of chattering birds, wandering fog and church bells ringing all around her, it's no wonder that Bea became a writer and storyteller.

ABOVE: Parrots can frequently be viewed from the porches at Harmony Hill.

RIGHT: The vintage Chinese garden chairs are hand-painted with ink-wash illustrations.

OVERLEAF: The sparkling lights of the Bay Bridge and the San Francisco skyline are a dramatic part of the Harmony Hill experience. The pillow is from J Thomas Design.

Porches for Earth and Sky

PAULA AND GLENN WALLACE — SAVANNAH, GEORGIA

Our 1890 bay-front row house, nestled on a corner in Savannah's famed Historic District, had neither a side garden nor a porch when my husband, Glenn, and I began restoring it. The preservation of a carriage house on the same property provided the impetus for creating two outdoor sanctuaries for us and our children, as well as many guests.

Porches create connections to people, to nature, to indoor worlds. Glenn and I incorporated comfort and style into our outdoor spaces. Like most busy families, mine prefers to use the back door rather than the front to enter the house. The side garden acts as a passageway, a portal between our busy professional lives and our cozy, familial one. Our goings are buoyed by the piquant whiffs of basil and rosemary snuggled in terra-cotta jars hung in winding, vintage wrought-iron trees. Our comings are guided by the softness of gas sconces outside the back porch, which envelop us in their glow.

From the main house, we access this secluded pocket garden through French doors flanking the dining room fireplace. The

LEFT: A cushioned basket swing from Thailand is an ideal place to enjoy the sounds of the city. A peeling sculpture "lounging" in the chaise adds artistry and whimsy.

OPPOSITE: Guests gravitate to this second-story aerie, the perfect spot for conversation or an après-dinner drink. It's protected from the elements by translucent corrugated roofing above the shuttered ceiling. Plants, glass vases, paintings and a thick-cushioned Lloyd-Flanders sofa create an appealing and inviting space.

LEFT: Our French bulldog, Molly, perched on an all-weather wrought-iron chair, enjoys both the view of the lush garden and the cool breeze of oscillating fans. A decorative metal *chapeau* that once formally announced a shop brings the eye upward for a touch of color.

BELOW: My family and I love to use fresh herbs plucked from their pots on the wall when we have casual suppers on the porch. Vintage tablecloths handed down by my mother add a sentimental touch.

addition of an eleven-foot-tall screened porch, just off the breakfast room, artfully expands our living space. Two skylights add an airiness and lightness that keep the room from feeling small, as do the whitewashed brick walls, which began life in the same deep red as the outside walls.

The thoughtful layout allows for a marriage of space and function, with the living room, den, and breakfast room all joining in unity to create a downstairs that invites family and friends to mingle and ensures that one can always be part of the conversation. Guests move inside and out, using the courtyard, garden, and back porch in their serpentine dance.

Glenn and I treasure the time we spend on the porch with our children, relaxing amid the winding topiaries and the verdant fig ivy that meanders up the exterior walls. We often have casual family suppers here, accented by the fragrant tea olive breeze kept blowing through strategically placed oscillating fans. Tea candles sprinkled on the table and pillar candles in scattered lanterns twinkle softly, adding a festive and magical glow to the nights.

Our porch blurs the distinction between inside and out with its tall screens and skylights. Vintage tablecloths handed down by my mother and bright red kimono pillows harmonize with seasonal flowers that fleck the garden. And because Glenn and I believe homes should have a sense of playfulness, an eclectic mix of art and furniture—a whimsical painting of two small boys in tall chairs by SCAD alumna Rose Casterline, a decorative red metal *chapeau* from Provence, and side tables made out of urns from the collection of designer Tom Leddy—helps keep the mood light and relaxing, and guests entertained as they explore our assembled vignettes.

The upstairs porch, sandwiched between four bedrooms in the main house and a small carriage house behind, offers an open-air view into the city while allowing us and our guests to remain secluded in our uptown outdoor sanctuary. Partygoers often wander upstairs for a tête-à-tête, gazing over rooftops or finding cushioned seating on which to share a glass of wine and peals of laughter. Teak chaises stretch out for private sunning during the day.

On cloudy days, the upstairs porch is the ideal place to watch storms creep in. The ceiling, made of louvered shutters, is topped with corrugated translucent roofing and outfitted with a misting system, sheltering us from the rain and providing a cool sultan-in-the-city environment—perfect for reading or just sipping iced tea.

An all-weather sisal rug topped by a faux zebra hide adds texture, defines the conversation nook and lends a touch of the exotic. To help create balance and harmony, Glenn and I repurposed a dormer window and outfitted it with a mirror, hung to face outside. According to feng shui principles, this position means the hustle and bustle of the street will bounce back and out of your house, leaving you serene and relaxed. And I'd have to say it works. Both porches, upstairs and down, are party-ready private havens.

BELOW: At night, a soft glow illuminates the garden. Often, we stop and sit, enjoying the whiffs of tea olives, the sounds of birds, the feel of grass and cool stone under our feet and the sight of fig ivy that has crept up the walls.

An Ashland Park Porch and Solarium

DEBBIE AND TONY CHAMBLIN — LEXINGTON, KENTUCKY

A century ago, a portion of Kentucky statesman Henry Clay's 600-acre estate was reinvented by the Olmsted brothers—sons of the legendary landscape architect Frederick Law Olmsted and acclaimed designers in their own right, having designed the grounds for the White House in addition to other esteemed projects. Among the surviving Olmsted signatures in the Lexington suburb known as Ashland Park are broad tree-lined roadways gently curved to offer sweeping vistas. From the front and back porches gracing the 1908 Dutch Colonial Revival home of Debbie and Tony Chamblin, the shaded views of the enclave's preserved houses are akin to peaceful visits to another era.

The area has eased into perfect harmony with nature thanks, in part, to limestone-rich soil that helps horses from these parts grow strong bones, and proves to be a friend to the native foliage as well. A majestic 300-year-old blue ash towers over the lawn next door, and additional noble specimens—sugar maple, sweet gum, yellow poplar and grand pin oaks—thrive throughout the neighborhood. "Ashland Avenue is one of the oldest residential streets in Lexington, so our window and porch views are all of

LEFT: A vintage wicker drinks cart carries a seltzer bottle and Moser glasses; Tony's "perfect Manhattans" made with Kentucky bourbon add a splash of color.

OPPOSITE: The porch features an original bead-board ceiling, a cement floor with a rim of glazed tiles and rusticated limestone bays.

mature trees," says Debbie. Notes local arborist Dave Leonard, "Mail carriers fight over those routes because they say working here is like walking in the woods!"

The Chamblins' home is meticulously preserved, with an L-shaped porch that retains many of its original details including a bead-board ceiling and a concrete floor rimmed in one-inch glazed tiles surrounded by five Kentucky River limestone bays of rusticated masonry. Each bay frames a lush Boston fern from March through October, when potted annuals and succulents are also placed on tables and around the wicker furnishings creating a friendly outdoor room where the couple can read the paper with their morning coffee or rest at day's end.

The Chamblins have lovingly enlivened their porch with treasures amassed during decades of scouting in Europe for their antique store, Belle Maison. Ten pieces of Bar Harbor and Art Deco wicker furniture are accented with the likes of antique

ABOVE: Scalamandré's Seashell Baroque in mint from the Island Cloth collection adds gentle color and texture to this wicker seating. A vintage glass cloche bell jar protects coral and shells that echo those in the fabric. The glass top on the wicker table protects it from rain and spills and allows glasses to sit flat.

LEFT: The solarium addresses the pool and terraced dining area; the glazing and brass fixtures are all original to the property.

binoculars and vintage seltzer bottles on a wicker drinks cart. A glass bell jar on the dining table protects a variety of treasures collected over the course of a season, including seashells and corals like those depicted in the Scalamandré fabrics on the chairs.

At the back of the house, the solarium is a self-contained wonder, with original paned glass and brass fixtures. It's a quiet, sunny spot on a wintry day, and a jewel-like room in any season, thanks to the collection of shell-encrusted decor by local artist Ron Meece. The view to the pool and flagstone patio is flanked by towering pines, swaying in the breeze and adding sheltered privacy.

Whether at the front or back of the house, in the immediate space furnished by the Chamblins, or in the heritage-rich avenue of homes and trees beyond their lawn, comfort and beauty abound. As stewards of this noble neighborhood, Debbie and Tony keep its flame and share its warmth. "We're fortunate to be part of such a historic community, and to be surrounded by home owners who are so committed to the care of the houses," she says.

ABOVE: Romeo the ornamental goldfish swims around a fishbowl resting on a stand created by Lexington artist Ron Meece. Though trained as a historic preservationist, Meece likes working with shells since "each piece has a life of its own."

CENTER: Coral adds a complementary white-on-white texture to the wicker table.

RIGHT: Collected by Debbie in France, this patinated trio of binoculars indicates the many hands and eyes that witnessed untold events over the past century.

Midnight on a
Monterey Square Porch

CAROLINE AND ED HILL — SAVANNAH, GEORGIA

Georgia natives Caroline and Ed Hill have watched the astonishing renaissance of downtown Savannah from a trio of the finest porches in town. Indeed, they played a part by restoring their own historic Monterey Square property.

The Hills are only the second family to reside in the structure as a single-family home; when they purchased it in 1978, the four floors and carriage house had been divided into seven apartments, plus a Bible warehouse and a dental lab. Nailing down details for the restoration demanded a decades-long dialogue with historians, carpenters and artisans. There was one key act of God as well: in 1979, the upper and lower side porches were relieved of their copper screening when Hurricane David blustered through "and ripped it all out," exclaims Ed. "I'm sure the neighbors had been seeing things they shouldn't when we had parties—the screens gave us a false sense of privacy."

The property has a colorful history, once serving as a beer garden and museum with "scientific" exhibits including three-headed chickens. Later, in a more elegant era, former

LEFT: The pierced brass lamps are dotted with orange and blue glass, sending flower-like patterns across the porches.

OPPOSITE: Antique kilim rugs soften the look of the original tongue-and-groove decking and add to the exotic flair provided by the Moroccan lamps that hang from the coffered ceiling, conjuring a colonial 1920s lifestyle in this nineteenth-century town home. A Buddhist shrine from The Paris Market offers a unique pedestal for candles.

Confederacy president Jefferson Davis and his daughter, Winnie, were guests in the home on the occasion of the grand opening of the Telfair Museum, the first art museum in the South. Today, the Renaissance Revival façade again appears as it did when Hugh Moss Comer, a president of the city's Cotton Exchange, built the stucco-on-brick structure in 1880. From the nine-foot cypress louvered shutters to the intricately carved heart pine balusters, and from the tongue-and-groove decking to the coffered ceiling in ivory, chocolate and golden Charleston brown (the tones that gave the woodwork from this era its "gingerbread" moniker), the construction and detailing are exquisite. A team of renovators removed a century's worth of lead paint that was clogging the open scrolls of the decorative woodwork,

LEFT: The set of six Moroccan pendant lamps offers a depth of atmosphere unmatched in Savannah's Historic District, yet is wholly appropriate for the city's colorful reputation; the patterns of light that the piercings create echo the arabesques in the decorative woodwork.

ABOVE: Dado saw-cut gingerbread balustrades and corbels offer texture and pattern, while still allowing the breezes to flow (and offering a bit of privacy).

thus restoring their delicacy before repainting every inch of the curls and hearts (using the historic colors) across hundreds of feet of balustrades and ornamentation enclosing the small front and two side porches. The historic Mercer Williams House, a neighboring local landmark where *Midnight in the Garden of Good and Evil*'s Jim Williams lived, occupies one of the other corner lots on the same square. Crowds increased dramatically after both homes were featured in the film adaptation of the book. Since the Hill residence overlooks this tourist circuit of trolleys, hansom cabs and pedestrian traffic, the couple enclosed their side yard with a garden wall. In the process, they added a small pool for koi and a host of potted plants, such as a Hong Kong orchid tree and Confederate Rose hibiscus. Mixed with the leafy green of the moss-draped live oaks in the square, the surroundings feel surprisingly tranquil—and private.

Morning light is blinding on the porches, so the couple typically avoid them until after noon. Since the home was not air-conditioned when they purchased it, the Hills got in the habit of retreating to the porches to escape the heat. Instead of French doors, the old double-hung windows extend all the way down to the floorboards, transitioning between indoors and out as they allow gentle passage between the two.

A spectacular ensemble of six bronze Moroccan pendant lanterns hangs from the coffered porch ceilings, complementing the arabesques in the gingerbread work and projecting swirls of colored light on the walls. The couple air colorful kilim carpets and pillows on the lower porch, which is also candlelit on occasion to evoke the indulgent pleasures of magnolia-scented antebellum nights. Unfortunately, exhaust from passing traffic necessitates that more delicate decor like the textiles cannot always remain outdoors, although the metal chairs and tables do. For impromptu parties, Ed says he prefers instead to invite lots of people so that "*they* become the decorations!"

BELOW: A vintage brass Moroccan bowl presents pistachios while a rattan-wrapped carafe holds lemonade.

BOTTOM: For festive occasions, colorful textiles, including a host of pillows, are added to the cast-metal furnishings.

OPPOSITE: With floor-to-ceiling double-hung windows, the inside and outside worlds are a continuum. The renovation team applied molding in chocolate and Charleston brown to the façade, enriching the intricacy; the term "gingerbread" was inspired by these shades of brown.

WATERFRONT PORCHES

With 180-degree views of Lake Fairlee, Suzy and Gordon Kerr's Vermont home is immersed in rippling light. The house is built into the shoreline's slope to keep their porches and living areas as close to the water's surface as possible.

Villa Allegra

ILONA AND CHAD OPPENHEIM — MIAMI BEACH, FLORIDA

Architect Chad Oppenheim speaks of certain Venetian qualities emanating from the home he shares with his wife, Ilona, a Swiss-born graphic designer and budding restaurateur, and their young son. The beauty and privacy of this canal-bordered home, the ease of walking to so many restaurants and shops and their ability to row in the moonlight right from the dock out to Biscayne Bay evoke the famed "city of water." Venetian architects have long hailed the canals and lagoon surrounding their villas as vital elements in their work; the way the light on the water reflects up onto every surface makes the entire city seem afloat. This "Ca' d'Oppenheim" demonstrates a similar oneness with its all-white walls, brilliant in the aquatic tropical light, and its ultramodern angles, which are softened by the play of shadows created by passing clouds and swaying fronds and leaves.

The Oppenheims never intended to become so attached to this white stucco home they had purchased as an investment, but when they saw the results of the 9,000-square-foot masterpiece's renovation, they couldn't bear to part with it. Building upon two walls and the general foundation from the original 1950s ranch house, the structure was remodeled, or better, reimagined, to

LEFT: Chad selected keystone, a highly textured coral rock quarried in the Florida Keys, for the front and rear façades of Villa Allegra.

OPPOSITE: Billowing two-story drapes add to the drama and romance. The white Pop chairs are by Tokoshin.

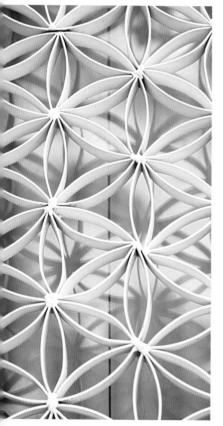

accentuate a warm and comfortable tropical modernism. Like simmering a sauce until it has reduced, Chad says, achieving the look meant getting rid of "everything that distracted from the pure essence." The house is simultaneously a world apart and in perfect harmony with South Florida, thanks to its materials, landscaping and architectural style, which the award-winning designer describes as romantic minimalism.

Beginning at the front privacy hedge, visitors to the property float through six zones Chad describes as experiential chambers. Each has its own subtly distinct personality, and each builds on the drama of the others. The parking court just off the road is paved with a checkerboard of clipped grass and rectangular blocks of keystone—a coral rock quarried in the Keys that's studded with seashells and fossilized plants. Up four steps and partly concealed behind billowing twenty-foot-tall drapes is a broad double-height entrance, the front façade of which is covered in a keystone veneer. Its wide window to the sky is mirrored by a rectangular reflecting pool of similar dimensions set into the coral stone floor directly beneath. The pierced roof transforms what might have simply been a courtyard into an intimate, while still quite modern, porch.

Passing through the foyer, which features a spectacular flight of floating cantilevered stairs, the next chamber is the combined living and dining space, which provides a water view, thanks to six

ABOVE: On warm evenings, Odegard's Indian marble table and benches with their matching candlesticks, plates and goblets stay cool to the touch.

LEFT: The Flower of Life metal railings on the master bedroom's balcony are an homage to Miami's Deco aesthetic. The hand-welded aluminum is a noncorrosive choice for this maritime environment.

PRECEDING PAGES: Villa Allegra is a "box of light," with dramatic shadows cast courtesy of recessed lighting in the ipe decking. The Basse Terre sofa is by Christian Liaigre with canvas-weave Perennials outdoor fabric; the coffee table is also by Liaigre. The hand-carved sandstone Vaso Africa planter is by Enzo Enea.

sets of French doors. Outside those doors, the rear façade of the soaring twenty-foot porch is also covered in the highly textured keystone veneer, "bookending" the home in this ancient rock and rooting it in its South Florida landscape. Durable Brazilian ipe wood floorboards radiate a high-gloss finish indoors but remain simply weather-treated on the porch, their chocolate tone adding a warm counterpoint to the cool white exterior.

This canal-facing porch is like an outdoor stage sparingly furnished with a carved Indian marble table and benches that stay cool to the touch on even the hottest evenings. Sofas and a chaise with easy-care canvas-covered cushions flank the coffee table by Christian Liaigre. Recessed into the floors, unobtrusive fixtures offer dramatic uplighting, throwing lively shadows onto the walls. For special occasions, flickering flames from hundreds of votive candles further enhance the glow. A balcony off the master bedroom offers views onto the scene below and out to the canal.

At the center of the sixty-foot expanse, a singular stucco structural column that doubles as an outdoor shower hoists the roof. Its interior is open to the sky; on sultry summer nights, it offers an invigorating ablution that becomes only more inspired when the full moon centers itself over the opening. (Upon visiting, architect Zaha Hadid termed the space "Chad's personal Pantheon.")

Three varieties of jasmine perfume the property, while a grass-rimmed infinity pool punctuates the emerald rear lawn within its border of trees for shade and privacy. Working with landscape architect Robert Parsley, the Oppenheims selected each specimen—sable palm, oleander, sea grape—to "create a natural environment that was true to the coast," Chad says.

Now, whether it's breakfast served on trays, supper after their son is asleep, a museum fund-raiser or a seated New Year's Eve dinner party for twenty-five, the house serves as a stunning complement to la dolce vita. "My favorite view of the house is when I'm sitting in the pool in the evening, looking at this box of light," Chad says. "As an architect it's hard to turn off your critical eyes, but with this house, I'm perfectly satisfied—it's one of my proudest moments."

BELOW: A structural column in the middle of the back porch conceals a two-story open shower that frames the passing clouds (and occasionally, the moon).

A Hill Country Hacienda

WEST KERR COUNTY, TEXAS

The lady of this house was accustomed to her mother's lifelong prefer-
ence for fine Louis XIV satins and gilding, but chose rustic Mexican
leather, iron and wood for her own home. Add in a family history in
Texas that includes land grants issued by the Spanish crown and a
decades-long love affair with the Mexican colonial city of Dolores
Hidalgo, and the style of this contemporary north-of-the-border
hacienda seems something like destiny.

The couple's deep Texas roots meant that when it came time to
build a retirement home, they didn't look for property outside of the
state as others might. Determined to settle in the Hill Country, they
visited many rolling acres in the area before choosing to build within
a grove of cypress, pecan and Spanish oak trees on a bucolic ranch
bordering Johnson Creek in west Kerr County.

The hospitality that the finished home
expresses draws many friends to its doors,
which suits the couple's warm and welcoming
nature. With its walls of native Cantera stone
and a flowing layout, architect Gale Garth
Carroll's design represents the best of the Lone

LEFT: The screened porch of the home
borders Johnson Creek and is shaded from
the Texan sun by pecan, cypress and oak trees.

OPPOSITE: The sunny terra-cotta-tiled
portico is decorated with a Jan Barboglio
standing candelabra and an antique armoire
filled with Mexican Catrina dolls—skeletons
dressed in folk costumes that are part of the
November 1 Day of the Dead celebration.

Star State's comfort and proportions colored by an air of the exotic world farther south. The house, designed to the couple's specifications as a hacienda with an open floor plan that keeps the air and guests circulating, reflects a remarkable combination of the grand with the down-home. Whether hundreds appear for charity auctions or twelve gather for elegant dinner parties, the gracious but relaxed mood of this home all but guarantees that a good time will be had by all.

On casual weekends, the hacienda's arcades and spacious living areas recall for houseguests the ease and restorative freedom of vacationing in San Miguel de Allende. The floors are of cool D'Hanis

LEFT: Dinners are frequently served on the porch at multiple tables.

BELOW: A ceramic dinner service by Guanajuato artist Gorky Gonzalez commemorates El Día de los Muertos, the Day of the Dead, but is used throughout the year.

terra-cotta tiles handmade in nearby San Antonio. Appended to the back of the hacienda, the gracious 950-square-foot screened porch is paved in those same tiles. With its beamed ceiling and cedar trusses, the porch proves a worthy backdrop for a stunning collection of Mexican furniture and decorative accents.

Corpus Christi–based interior designer Susie Rucker helped deploy the variety of colorful objects that tell stories on every surface. A fringed shawl on a chair near the fireplace and a framed vintage *huipil* poncho over the mantel soften the environment, while silver *milagros* mounted on the pine armoire are gentle reminders of injured family members in need of meditation and prayer.

Representing more than a quarter century of collecting, a panoply of crosses features metal, clay and even driftwood to subtly and simply carry the message of faith and sacrifice. Throughout the year, a primitive Texan birthing chair sits near a sculpture of the peacefully smiling Virgin of Cocharcas. During the holidays, scores of nativity scenes appear on tables and chests to recall miracles; an entire room is devoted to storing these figures during the rest of the year.

Rucker accompanied the couple to El Paso to direct the creation of custom wrought-iron accents, including chandeliers; the broad candelabra that shines down from the carved wooden mantel traveled from San Miguel; Texas artisan Jan Barboglio's pair of iron hurricane candles and a standing candelabra complement the stone and wood. All manner of craftsmanship is illuminated by the candles and firelight in the evenings and shaded from the mighty Texan sun all day.

Each of the natural elements—earth, fire, water, air—is present here. The breeze that flows so freely is easy to enjoy from many welcoming perches on the porch. And then there are the springing sika and grazing axis deer, and occasional flocks of turkeys just beyond the screens—as well as the sound, just a stone's throw away, of the winding creek that rushes out to feed the Guadalupe River, and nourishes the spirits of all those who hear it.

BELOW: Tucked next to a shawl-covered armchair, the Virgin of Cocharcas from Peru is the queen of the heavens and the waters; she blesses and protects farmers and their harvest, apropos here on a creek-bordered ranch.

RIGHT: The framed textile above the fireplace is a *huipil* from Guanajuato, a traditional poncho worn by women in central and southern Mexico; the textile pattern indicates where the woman is from, much like the tartan plaids of Scotland announce their clans. An antique birthing chair sits in front of the fire. The carved wood mantel is from outside Dolores Hidalgo; the hurricane candles are by Jan Barboglio.

OPPOSITE, ABOVE: A few of the many crosses collected by the lady of the house. The green pineapple sculpture is a *piña* from Patambán, Michoacán; made from low-fired red clay, *piñas* are traditionally glazed in blue, green or ochre.

OPPOSITE, BELOW: The *milagros* ("miracles") hung on the pine armoire are an entreaty for the cure of an injured leg, a recovery from carpal tunnel from years of needlepointing, the safeguard of a child or the petition for other special intentions. Eventually, the entire surface will be covered as stories and events unfold in the family's life.

The Porches at Snake Ravine

ARTHUR ROGER — POPLARVILLE, MISSISSIPPI

Even mapping devices sometimes fail to guide the way to Arthur Roger's secluded weekend retreat. The circuitous route over interstates, blacktop county roads, a macadam lane and a rutted dirt trail through a Mississippi forest includes miles without stop signs or lights. When the semicircular drive is reached at last, a walk across a manicured pine-needle path leads to a sudden view of the house and a slender wooden bridge that spans a dry creek bed. The bridge is precisely angled toward an open porch area that separates the public areas of the house from the private living quarters.

The tortuous trail is intentional. "I wanted to build a sense of adventure with this house—that it wasn't just about transferring all the comforts of the city to a home in the woods, but that it would be like coming to camp," Arthur explains. A prominent gallery owner in New Orleans during the business week, he wanted this weekend hideaway to offer a lifestyle far removed from that in his historic French Quarter residence and warehouse district gallery. After glamorous show openings, discussions with artists and negotiations with buyers, it's a pleasant change of pace to come here and be serene.

LEFT: A pine-decked, cable-railinged bridge dramatically carries visitors toward the house. It was constructed to shake a bit with the foot traffic, adding to the spirit of adventure Arthur envisioned.

OPPOSITE: Hurricane Katrina's eye passed directly over Poplarville in 2005. It took three months to chop through the fallen trees, but there was virtually no damage to the Wellington Reiter-designed house itself.

Part of that mind-set includes as much contact with nature as possible, so porches were a primary consideration when Arthur collaborated with architect (and current president of the School of the Art Institute of Chicago) Wellington Reiter on the design for the 2,000-square-foot home in 1997.

Situated on a 12-acre lot bordered by the Wolf River, the house was carefully positioned to take full advantage of the heavily forested setting and quietude that the trees provide. The two men instinctively decided to elevate the home well above a ravine, positioning the outdoor spaces to catch the light and breezes. Not surprisingly, wood was selected as the primary structural and surface material, with strategically placed steel bracing used to make the house as visually delicate as possible. However, while the appearance is elegant and spare, the steel members and braided-wire cabling allowed the house to resist the destructive forces of Hurricane Katrina's 175-mile-per-hour winds and the resulting twenty-foot storm surge.

Like the deck of a ship, the back porch launches toward the river with teak-topped tension cable railings and stained-pine decking. Sparsely furnished with a canvas-covered daybed that's suspended by steel cables from the sixteen-foot ceiling, the platform is a perfect vantage point for watching the sun set or friends paddling in the river, or for gazing through Jesús Moroles's granite *Spiral Disc* to the ironwood and beech trees beyond.

While the interior space buzzes with stimulating works by artists Arthur represents, including Dale Chihuly, Francis X. Pavy and Clyde Connell, the exterior of the home mainly relies upon the trees, river and sky as its focal points. Only a few works of art punctuate the simplicity of the surroundings. Years of walks along the white-sand shores of the river have yielded a

BELOW: On the back porch, *Spiral Disc*, a work in granite by artist Jesús Moroles—inspired by the work he created for the Beijing Olympics—is boldly suspended by ropes, creating a focused frame through which to view the forest beyond. Arial, a basset hound-chocolate lab mix, surveys the scene.

collection of "holes with rocks around them" and petrified wood that Arthur displays in an untreated wood frame on the front porch's wall. The collection is both artful and indicative of the state of mind that he reaches here—one of meditation and calm consideration. It's a perfect welcome sign in this hub space joining the three wings of the house, where guests are greeted and everyone gears up for hikes.

Arthur purchased the property after spending several years visiting the area with friends on weekends. Just ninety minutes from New Orleans, the town is a popular country destination for city folks, but unlike other metropolitan getaway areas, this one isn't about the social scene, restaurants or shopping. "In general, people keep to themselves when they visit their homes here—we stock up and hunker down, gardening, chopping wood and just enjoying the peace, quiet and beauty of the woods," says Arthur. "The funny thing is, all the things I hate doing in the city—yard work, cooking every night—I look forward to doing here as a kind of therapy. Of course, at first I had this impulse to try to organize nature with all that activity—but the hurricane cured me of that!"

ABOVE: The house has three living areas that converge here at the front porch. Working Class Studio's all-season pillows designed by Andrea Gray accent a wooden bench. During his riverside walks Arthur collects "holes with rocks around them" and pieces of petrified wood (seen in the framed piece above the bench).

RIGHT: A trio of shovels created by Neil Hartford with found wood handles and blades of rolled glass is a perfect complement to the spirit of working with nature that pervades this home.

A Camp Porch

NANCY AND JIM HUGHES — WEST FAIRLEE, VERMONT

The forest ringing Lake Fairlee has been audience to many sounds over the ages, including the calls of moose and eagles, the conversations of the Penobscot nation and the songs of summer campers. Arias from *Tosca* remain, however, something of a surprise in these woods. "Many a summer night we'll be singing opera out on the porch, accompanied by Jim on the piano, or listening to him perform solo," Nancy Hughes says with a smile of admiration for her husband. "Jim's grandmother was a classically trained singer—he inherited her gifts."

Singing, picnicking and reading are all standard fare for campers. But on Jim and Nancy's lakeside porch, those relaxed activities take on a decidedly grown-up feel. Where comic books were once read under covers with flashlights by young campers, the book club begun by Nancy in Washington, D.C., still meets once a year. Instead of fire-roasted marshmallows and hot dogs, guests find political discussions fueled by potluck parties of salad, gourmet

LEFT: Lake Fairlee flows into the Connecticut River on its way to the sea. "In winter, we love the sound of the cracking ice echoing across the lake as it freezes and squeezes itself together—it sings," says Nancy.

OPPOSITE: Sam, Passumpsic Point's Casanova, watches geese, cardinals and chickadees from his perch. The porch isn't screened because "it's high enough above the ground that we aren't bothered by the bugs," Nancy explains. In the background are a pair of the original fir bark-clad camp cabins, now used for visiting grandchildren.

bread and cheese. But while the conversations might be lofty, the clean lines of sturdy plank benches and an old farm table maintain a carefree atmosphere, where there's always a place for one more.

Their plot of earth wasn't always so civilized. A century ago, New York high school teacher Harvey Newcomer wrapped himself in buffalo robes on a wintry day to explore by horse-drawn sleigh what was then a sheep farm. He deemed the land on this point jutting into the lake to be the ideal spot for children to be tested by nature in a place insulated from urban epidemics. In 1914, Newcomer established Camp Passumpsic, one of nine sleepaway camps that lined the six-mile lakeshore.

Nancy and Jim purchased Newcomer's property in the early 1980s, first as a summer home. The couple loved the look and ease of the old counselors' cabin with its open westward-facing porch standing among the oaks, birches and maples. Ultimately, though, the building, constructed as it was for summer camp use, needed too many changes to be considered a comfortable residence, but it was salvaged out of respect for its history. After relocating the old cabin farther from the shore, architect Clark Graff built the new house to the identical design with slightly larger proportions (and more modern plumbing, electricity and fixtures) on the same spot, naturally including the open porch facing the lake.

The central decorative feature on the porch is an antique wooden cabinet brimming with vintage milk and cream bottles. It serves as a reminder of the busy days the Hughes children spent digging for treasures all over their former home in Norwich—and the legacy of dairy farms in Vermont and New Hampshire. Their glass shapes and nostalgic lettering add to the bygone-era comfort.

The pace of life on the point encourages low-key visits with family and friends while also allowing Nancy and Jim to remain active in their retirement by sailing, hiking and cross-country skiing. Along their water and land routes, they're treated to endless entertainment provided by muskrats, cormorants and cardinals. In the summer, their porch view includes boaters and swimmers, while in winter it's the ice fishermen who arrive in search of pike, as skaters cut graceful lines into the fifteen-inch-thick sheet around them. What was once a summer home is now a year-round residence for Jim and Nancy, but the feeling of being on vacation never fades.

BELOW: Bottles mainly from Vermont and New Hampshire dairies unearthed by the three Hughes sons stand resplendent in the pure mountain light.

OPPOSITE: Cyclamen and chicken foot thrive atop an antique set of drawers while a cushioned rush-seated rocker offers a comfortable spot from which to view the lake. The all-wood, earth-toned walls, ceiling and decking are in perfect harmony with their forest home.

A D-I-Y Porch

MARIA AND RAFAEL LOPEZ — MIAMI LAKES, FLORIDA

Interior stylist Maria Molinari is delighted to stay at home. "People travel to southern Florida for vacation, so why would we want to leave?" she asks. Though the presence of her husband Rafael Lopez's family members in the area influenced their decision, the opportunity for lakeside living—and fishing for peacock bass from the back lawn—was a major draw. But it was the 530-square-foot screened porch with a view of the water that sealed the real estate deal for this family.

With son Tomas, now twenty-one, the couple settled on one of twenty-three man-made bodies of water in Miami Lakes, a 1960s community with curving tree-lined streets. The neighborhood was an early example of what has come to be called New Urbanism—meaning, in part, that shops and restaurants are both within walking distance. "We might have bought a home that was more modernized, but we couldn't imagine a better view in such a great community," says Maria.

LEFT: An outdoor shower located just outside one of two porch doors is a refreshing summer convenience after swimming in or boating on Lake Sarah.

OPPOSITE: Maria designed the platform daybeds to preserve the view of the lake from the interior rooms; six skylights keep the space bright even on overcast days. Gauzy curtains on bamboo rods add privacy and obscure the screens without blocking the light.

LEFT: Lake breezes blow through the screened porch into the master bedroom through French doors.

OPPOSITE, ABOVE: The pair of twelve-foot-long platforms accommodate twin mattresses with enough overhang to use as extra seating or end tables. Color and texture are introduced by toss pillows from Peking Handicraft.

OPPOSITE, BELOW: The porch is perfect for casual dinners (as well as poker games).

Neither she nor Rafael, a financier, had much do-it-yourself experience. Fortunately, the leaking roof and dark rooms of the ranch house on Lake Sarah brought out their inner contractors, offering ample opportunities for creativity. Hanging drywall, painting, rewiring, installing a new shower just outside the porch—there seems to be no limit to what the two have proven themselves capable of tackling.

The previous owners had invested in buff-colored ceramic tile floors, limestone columns and a stainless steel grill for the porch, so the couple spent less than $2,500 in furnishing the space to their tastes. They added ceiling fans; a wooden chest of drawers from their friend, artist Perez Celis; a table and chairs; and such decorative accents as banana palm fiber vases, candles and pillows.

The couple faced one vexing design challenge: how to add seating without interrupting the lake view from the living room. After considering countless sofas and chairs, Maria came up with her own design for platform daybeds one long evening while her husband was engrossed in a *Twilight Zone* marathon. "I was losing my mind, and needed a distraction!" she explains.

The trim L-shaped lounge beds hover just nine inches above the cool floor tiles. "Headboards" keep the playfully mismatched collection of toss pillows from slipping behind the twin mattresses clad in custom slipcovers. She built the platforms from stained plywood, using leftover material to create a coffee table fitted with a skirt of bamboo beach mats. Because the twelve-foot bed platforms are much longer than the mattresses, they also offer occasional seating and serve as end tables.

The porch accounts for about a quarter of the family's living space nine months of the year. While relaxing on it, the couple watch for neighbors trawling along the shoreline in paddleboats ("usually seeking drink refills," Rafael quips). In summer, the porch can sometimes be too hot to use for afternoon naps, private dinners, cocktail parties with clients or Rafael's poker games with high school friends. But during the rest of the year, the couple's hospitality—to the beat of a sound track of his Cuban favorites and songs from her Argentinian father's tango CD—keeps things lively in this little piece of paradise.

An Antebellum River Porch

ELLEN AND SIDNEY JEFFERSON "JEEP" BOLCH —
VERNONBURG, GEORGIA

"When my husband and I were married and were joining our families, we needed a larger home to accommodate all of our children and their children, eventually. I knew I wanted to be on the water, but I didn't want just *any* water—I wanted to be part of a historic community," Ellen Bolch recalls. She got her wish when one of the few homes in Vernonburg became available. This gem of a township is home to a little more than one hundred people ("I honestly think they counted our Jack Russells in that census," Ellen jokes). It was settled by German craftsmen shortly after Savannah's founding in 1733 and has always been a kind of oasis along the deep and peaceful Vernon River, which leads to the Intracoastal Waterway.

The Bolches' 1847 foursquare Italianate home was built on an idyllic plot of land using mortise-and-tenon construction. In this ancient joined-wood method, tenons—which are carved from the

LEFT: An angel stands guard in the fountain in front of the road porch at the Bolch home. The double staircase is a traditional antebellum architectural feature; it's said that in gentler times, gentleman were not to gaze upon a lady's ankles as she lifted her skirts to ascend steps; as a mark of honor, gentlemen climbed one set of stairs, while ladies went up the other.

OPPOSITE: The heart pine boards of the river porch floor, bead-board ceiling, columns and railings are all original to the 1847 construction. The vast stretch of the porch is punctuated with plants and a variety of seating solutions.

end of a piece of timber—are inserted into the mortise, or cavity, of another, with no nails or adhesives, allowing the wood to expand or contract along with the humidity levels. Raised during the heyday of Savannah's lucrative cotton trade, the house is grand in style but comfortable in scale. The back porch (facing the road) features a double staircase that is a hallmark of antebellum Southern homes; it's said that as a matter of courtesy gentlemen were not to ascend stairs behind ladies, so they approached entrances from opposite sides.

When Ellen and her husband, Jeep, first looked at the property, the home was far from the perfectly preserved structure that now stands. "The steps were rotted through, there were cigar burns in the heart pine floors and there were *pigeons* living on the second floor!" Ellen recalls. Although the family has dispatched those pests, avian themes—in the form of birdcages as well as bird-watching on the porch—remain a leitmotif. Brown pelicans swoop across the water, great blue herons pluck koi fish from the pond ("Vernonburg's most expensive sushi," says Ellen) and bald eagles, hawks and wood storks are all in attendance, thanks in part to a bird island just around the bend in the river. The property also sports an unusual clock, which announces the setting of the sun: at day's end, a towering magnolia on the river lawn goes white as snowy egrets descend to roost for the evening just before the sun drops below the horizon. Further afield, dolphins play in the river, which is not only a sanctuary for wildlife but a playground for sailors, water-skiers and swimmers.

Some of the presences at the Bolch home, however, are distinctly less...corporal. When one of their renovators was working on the porch steps one evening, he felt someone or some*thing* push him—so forcefully that he had to catch himself, leaving him with the strong sense of a spirit eager to see the property restored properly. Ellen doesn't feel there is anything malevolent in the environment, but instead attributes these sensations to a

LEFT: The alligator sculpture on the river lawn isn't just a conversation piece; the prehistoric creatures are common to this region.

more general spirit that the house seems to have when there are many guests and lights blazing. "It has a *soul*," she says. "It shimmers more when there are lots of people here; there's a palpable sense that the house is happy."

The river porch is a veritable stage. Events performed here include Easter egg hunts, Lowcountry boils, petting zoo birthday parties and shows performed by the grandchildren after Thanksgiving dinner, with an adoring audience of grown-ups wrapped in faux fur blankets to stay warm.

Of all the gatherings that the porch has supported, one is clearly the theatrical winner: a family friend's wedding reception held in 2001, timed for the full moon reflecting on the high tide. "There isn't a lot of artifice to Vernonburg—people here grew up crabbing and swimming in the river—but there is a lot of beauty and history, with an undercurrent of surprise. We wanted the wedding to reflect this character—to celebrate it," says Ellen. The moon delivered a honey apricot glow over the whole Old South evening. The couple were presented on the river porch to the guests below, who were entertained with refreshments in a champagne, canapés and caviar tent. Orchids in birdcages served as centerpieces, while suspended lanterns in the live oaks and a trumpeter leading guests like the pied piper added to the celebratory mood.

But for all of its history and elegant soirees, the Bolch home doesn't take itself too seriously; Ellen has only two rules about the furniture: one, it has to survive the dogs, and two, it has to withstand feet being propped up. She's more likely to be found drinking a beer than a fancy cocktail or fine wine—although perhaps from a crystal glass. "To me, a porch is a place of great family comfort—and a marriage of being outside and being in."

ABOVE: The Bolch porches offer plentiful seating for their many guests. Ellen is a great lover of birds; the cage collection attests to her devotion to them, wild and domestic alike. She once placed a wooden dove in one of the birdcages as a decorative accent, and was surprised to see twigs and pine straw begin to appear—a real dove began to lay there.

LEFT: Multiple conversational areas allow for intimate and grand gatherings alike.

OPPOSITE, ABOVE: The canary, Tweet-Tweet, sings only when others are speaking or there's music playing; if the area is silent, so is he.

OPPOSITE, BELOW: The view to the dock on the Vernon River.

Riverfarm Nursery

SARA AND STEVEN PARADIS — GOSHEN, KENTUCKY

Steven Paradis is simply unstoppable. "My husband has so many brilliant ideas—every morning he's downstairs waiting to tell me the latest," laughs his wife, Sara. What started as a plan for a two-room duck hunting cabin at the family's Kentucky tree nursery became a sprawling 5,000-square-foot weekend residence. "I wasn't paying close enough attention when he started talking about this particular project; it just kept growing!" she exclaims.

A colorful cast of characters helped to realize Steven's vision. Bill Pace, a specialist in the sourcing and restoration of antique log structures, located the nineteenth-century poplar tobacco barn and white oak Amish cattle barn. The logs, which had been shipped in numbered pieces, were reassembled (the barn's "second raising") using the modern sealant Perma-Chink rather than the traditional mixture of hog hair, wood chips and lime putty. The reconstruction crew hired to join the barns together at the site included fifth-generation masons, who constructed limestone fireplaces and the stone interlude that joins the two cabins, as

LEFT: A vintage enamel washtub serves as a beer cooler, setting the tone at the top of the steps for arriving guests.

OPPOSITE: Copper porch flooring adds a unique sheen to this reconfigured Amish cattle barn. While grand in scale, the expansive porch actually reduced construction costs, freeing much of the timber frame from enclosure. A carved wooden gondola from a long-shuttered English amusement park overflows with a cargo of pillows sewn from cotton sacks.

well as a host of craftsmen and day laborers—some of them sculptors, others furniture makers and one a former guitarist for Hank Williams Jr.—who followed with floors and roofing. The team briefly included some local Amish carpenters, too. "They were the *workin'est* guys, making everybody else look bad!" Pace recalls.

Today, a two-story front porch offers visitors a distinctive welcome. Steven and Sara wasted no time putting the place to work hosting "outright outrageous hootenannies." Most of the music that gets played is homespun when the Paradis boys are home with their guitars and the guys from Kentucky's own Relic can be persuaded to hang around after a party. Pace or farm manager Ben Walter might join in, and Steven will always happily provide a solo on the blues harmonica or follow along on his Gibson Dobro or the antique Martin that belonged to Sara's father. "If you can't sing good, sing loud" is the Paradis porch philosophy, with company sitting around the outdoor fireplace wrapped up in quilts after the sun sets and everyone is silhouetted against the flames.

The massive log walls serve as a backdrop to rush-seated rockers paired with side tables created from vintage lard tins. Such down-to-earth furnishings function as a counterpoint to architectural elements like the triptych of soaring stained-glass windows that once graced an English church and a floral relief carving hung on the lintel of the fireplace. Sara, a treasure hunter since childhood, fills the spaces with colorful and inviting pieces. "I remember my first flea market, when I was young," she shares. "I bought a Sanka can full of marbles, and I wish I still had it!" Her funky collection delivers humor and comfort

RIGHT: The setting sun, the fireplace and electric lights silhouette the porch's timber frame.

OPPOSITE: A brass bed covered with vintage quilts is haloed by framed pictures obtained at yard sales or vintage shops. The "Quebec" hooked rug is a nod to the Paradis family's French Canadian heritage.

aplenty: there are chicken-leg candlesticks and a stuffed turkey (whose holiday outfits give new meaning to "dressing") as well as a 1920s enamel clothes washer brimming with ice and bottled beer, all of which hint at the good times possible here. In Steven's words, "The house has an energy that draws people to it."

Yet somehow, amid all the commotion of summer parties and busy holiday gatherings, the couple and their children also enjoy many quiet weekends. Hanging from the rafters, a dragon-headed gondola from a Lake District amusement park has become an inspired place for napping and dreaming. It's difficult to imagine a more tempting setting than the porch at sunset. One can read Mark Twain from the vantage point of an antique brass bed loaded with gently worn quilts as, below on the Ohio River, bellowing barges ply their way downriver toward the great Mississippi.

ABOVE: The unfinished wood banjo chair comes apart in two pieces to lie flat "so you can throw it in the back of the pickup," according to Steven.

RIGHT: "Organic farming on steroids" is how farm manager Ben Walter describes his Rudolf Steiner–developed biodynamic method. As is appropriate for his Kentucky heritage, Steven describes their modest initial plots as "small batch," while Sara calls them "an extension of our family culture"—healthy and supportive of the local community. Radishes, turnips, carrots and greens from the farm add resonant color to the porch.

OPPOSITE: The massive limestone fireplace warms the porch in spring and autumn. Sara dresses Steven's one-and-only turkey hunting trophy in horns for Halloween (and a Santa hat for Christmas, and...).

Passumpsic Point

SUZY AND GORDON KERR — WEST FAIRLEE, VERMONT

Suzy and Gordon Kerr's first home on this lakefront property was an 800-square-foot camp cabin that had been the seasonal lodging for the directors of the Passumpsic Boys' Camp. The couple used the simple one-bedroom log structure with a small kitchen and living room for nine years, finally supplementing it with a new guest cabin to accommodate family and friends. Built quite close to Lake Fairlee's shore, the cabin had a sensual relationship with the lake that later informed the design of the Kerrs' larger retirement residence, including the incorporation of porches and decks on every side, which would allow them to be near the lapping water and surrounding vistas through all stages of the sun's rising and setting.

"We built the house so that the first floor was cut back into the slope," Gordon explains. "We wanted that square footage, but we also wanted the main living areas to be as level with the lake's surface as possible." With 180-degree views of the lake and woods, light often bounces off the rippling surface into the home. The Norwich, Vermont, architectural firm of Smith & Vansant

LEFT: A Simon Pearce bowl on the lakefront porch's dining table holds Granny Smith apples and dried sunflowers. This screened porch off the dining room and kitchen is the main gathering place for the family.

OPPOSITE: A rush-seated rocking chair, with a throw by the New England mill Kennebunk, offers a comfortable nook for reading. The railings were designed to be broad enough to hold glasses and mugs of coffee. On the Fourth of July, fireworks are launched from the floating dock in the background.

employed a New England vernacular style so the house "would look as though it had been a part of the shoreline for at least fifty years," Gordon adds. Project architect Stephen Branchflower explains that "the dark low-gloss Englert steel roofing and bark-stained white cedar shingles were chosen to make the home blend in, so when it's seen from the water, it's in harmony with the forest."

Further, "the house was designed to follow the contours of Passumpic Point—the southern and western porches in particular take advantage of this orientation, so when you're standing on them, you feel like you're hovering above the water—or the ice, as the case may be," Stephen adds. All of the porches enhance the pleasures of a day at the lake. The back porch serves as the main entrance to the home, and from it the Kerrs watch their children and five grandchildren play croquet on the adjacent lawn. Off the living room, the "sunset" porch is a serene vantage point for the couple to unwind with their feet up, drinks in hand, as sailboats tack in at day's end. The floating dock to the left is the launching point for water-skiing adventures, and for the fireworks set off on the Fourth of July as well as on Suzy's birthday.

The Kerrs' flora and fauna show, viewed from the comfort of their rattan and rush-seated chairs, includes sightings of small-mouth bass leaping in the lake, bald eagles diving for fish and riots of autumn ash, maple and birch leaves tumbling to the forest floor. The screened porch provides perfect views of rising morning mists as kayakers, Canadian geese, beavers and otters cut through the water. Thanks to the protection of the steel screening, pesky blackflies are kept at bay, so the family also share informal evening meals here, never worrying about dress codes or spills on the table.

Life on Lake Fairlee is quite a paradigm shift from the pressures and social demands of Capitol Hill, where Suzy and Gordon spent most of their younger lives as a lobbyist and a senatorial chief of staff. The only preening and posturing in this neck of the woods come thanks to the resident loons, cormorants and egrets. "We chose this place for retirement by chance, really," Gordon marvels. His wife's former colleague, who lives next door, had suggested the couple visit while traveling from Canada to Maine on a route they had found in a *U.S. News & World Report* article about great scenic drives. Little did the Kerrs know they were actually heading home.

BELOW AND OPPOSITE: The Kerr's screened porch offers views onto the soft light of dawn, with fingers of mist rising from Lake Fairlee's tranquil surface. Throughout the year, the water is visited by fishermen, kayakers, ice-skaters and water-skiers as well as an array of wilder creatures, including eagles, bass, geese, muskrats and otters.

OVERLEAF: The "sunset" porch with its stone terrace extension is a perfect spot for watching boaters come in for the day, and for entertaining guests. Sustainable and weather-resistant canberra wood was used for the decking on most of the porches. The rattan chair and ottoman are by Pottery Barn.

COUNTRY PORCHES

At Linda and Tommy DeHennis's Glen Ellen, California, house, rustic bent-twig furniture is wholly at home with aboriginal art and architectural details inspired by those found in Australia.

The Neshoba County Fair

PHILADELPHIA, MISSISSIPPI

Among the gullies and red hills in the Magnolia State, no fewer than six hundred colorful wooden shacks line up like brownstones on a New York avenue. But these spirited little cottages—which have been passed down, knocked down and rebuilt by occupants since 1889—are a star attraction at the Neshoba County Fair for one week every July. Though not much bigger than a suburban shopping mall, the historic fairgrounds are crisscrossed by a web of intersecting paths and picturesque lanes shaded by oaks and pines.

Of course, each resident of the colony is convinced that his or her address is the best. Sid Salter, an editor of *The Clarion-Ledger*, Mississippi's largest newspaper, is a perfect example. Over those seven days, his popular porch is usually near capacity since his cabin lies adjacent to Founder's Square, right at the historic center of the fairgrounds. In the course of one hour, Salter might invite a half dozen visitors to lunch—including a few older gentlemen who have mistaken his

LEFT: Happy Hollow is one of the fair's quieter lanes, not much wider than a sidewalk. Residents haul in truckbeds full of sawdust from a nearby mill to keep the lanes dry after summer rains—and to give the little ones something to play in on long afternoons.

OPPOSITE: Fair porches are built for company. A bench has been added to the very edge of this one, jutting out just beyond the cover of the roof. Even though this fair's focus is family time, it does have its share of attractions and distractions: a Gravitron and a Ferris wheel can be seen in the background.

cabin for another. Salter also supplies the storytelling and the memories, not to mention the games of cops-and-robbers and live music that starts after sunset. It's akin to a rural Mardi Gras—less sensual and more domestic, but just as much fun. Maybe *more* fun. "Some families live from Christmas to Christmas," says Sid. "We live from fair to fair."

Myna Hooper's porch faces the racetrack and bandstand where, many moons ago, she was crowned the youngest-ever Miss Neshoba County Fair, at the tender age of fourteen. Now nearly seventy and almost blind, Hooper has memorized the route from her chair on the porch to the cooler and bar just inside the front door, where she makes a mean Bloody Mary. She calls her porch old-timey, wide-open and built for looking. "You can see everything worth seeing," she proclaims, "and it's more interesting than television." Arriving friend (and beauty pageant protégée Neldie Mooney) adds that "the entertainment is endless" as she ascends Hooper's steps. "And it's free!"

During fair week each summer, people climb onto one porch or another for a thousand good reasons—to catch up, to play some music or a hand of cards or for a drink and a story—until it's time to say good night. Around bedtime, the place quiets down just long enough for a little rest, and then comes another day.

The fair's porches are sometimes primitive in their simplicity, given their infrequent use, but they are seldom plain. Seating features prominently, from the obligatory porch swing and rockers to

built-in benches bounded by perimeter railings. Hooper's great-grandfather built her
cabin; she kept some of its wood to ensure
a bit of intergenerational continuity when
rebuilding it. "This is the original façade,
here," Myna says, gesturing to a wall behind
her. The old planks are painted with the
orange, green, yellow and blue of a crazy
quilt "overstitched" in black. "We had lots
of different colors of paint from my family's
general store in town," she explains. "So we
used them all!"

Today only a few of the little buildings
are weathered gray and brown. Others
display shades ranging from Pepto pink to
orange sherbet, grape soda and electric lime.
The fruit-flavored rainbow was started by
one Lallah Perry some six decades ago. Now
nearly ninety, Lallah took matters into her
own hands because "it looked like a prison
camp," she jokes. After painting her own
Happy Hollow Street cabin white, she added
drawings of flowers, people, sunsets and
landscapes. Redone every few years since,
her characters are rendered in bold primary colors and great Fauvist brushstrokes
as varied and cheerful as the fair itself.
Lallah's colorful clothing blends right into
the environment; she's as much a fixture
of her porch as the tables and chairs, and
is even more welcoming.

Fair porches advertise everything from cold
beverages to political candidates to favorite
Southern schools (opposite). Each of these
cabins has a coveted second-story porch,
high enough above the dust and the crowd to
offer a little more air and a lot more privacy.

RIGHT: Younger children spend their days at the fair playing on swings and in cribs on the porch while the older kids have more free rein. "There's no TV out here," says one fairgoer, "so there's nothing for them to do but play."

BELOW: Fairgoers on racetrack-facing porches can watch the horses but also music performances and the Miss Neshoba County Fair Pageant on the infield stage.

OPPOSITE: Lallah Perry, seated here on her Happy Hollow porch, is part of the reason the fair is exploding with color. As a recently married art student whose family had their own cabin, Lallah decided to add a little color to the whitewashed secondhand wood. She's been repainting her cabin every few years ever since.

A Frontier-Era Porch

DINAH AND JIM MARTIN — WACO, KENTUCKY

This rambling home, assembled from three Daniel Boone–era log cabins, is a dream come true for owners Dinah and Jim Martin. Raised in rural Kentucky, the two were introduced at nearby Berea College, where they were among the students who created Appalachian crafts in exchange for tuition. A local cow with milk fever deserves credit for bringing Jim, a veterinarian, to the couple's current Waco neighborhood years later. "In the end, the cow was healed and we'd found the land we'd been looking for, right next door to the farm," says Jim. Building on this patch of earth with its fishing pond, burning bush shrubs and grove of wild apple trees became one of the couple's favorite projects.

Noble old-growth oak and poplar trees were felled for the cabins' logs more than two hundred years ago; each length of wood was brought in, piece by piece, from cabins in eastern Kentucky counties. Today, the ancient wood retains all of its beauty from its earlier lives including the axe marks from the hewing, holes for rifles to poke through, and nail holes from when people tried to cover the logs with clapboards to "dress them up" in later eras. The master bedroom suite is a former mule barn; the other two

LEFT: Zella Wilson, a fellow member of the Waco Baptist Church, presented this etched gourd (grown on her farm) to the Martins as a housewarming present.

OPPOSITE: The front porch spans two of the three joined cabins. Vintage quilts are stacked on a church pew (left foreground), ready to warm the frequent visitors to the Martin porch, while split hickory rockers and benches offer their welcomes.

cabins from which the home was constructed shelter additional bedrooms as well as the common living and utility areas.

Like the home they grace, both the lower three-sided porch and the upper porch at the back of the home offer comfort and a rugged sense of frontier heritage. One log wall has a veritable gallery of antique objects that now seem quaint but were once tantamount to survival: iron salt-boiling pots, saws, cattle yokes, cooper's hoops, sheep shears, lanterns. The front length of the porch is also decorated with a church pew, etched gourds, Bybee Pottery spongewear (from the factory, which is just a mile away) and baskets woven by Berea artisans.

The couple's adoration for the region is apparent through front porch furnishings like the split-hickory rockers and benches. They were made by locals who pull the strips from the wood just beneath the trees' bark and form frames from the trunks and branches. The wooden swing is a favorite seat for the couple as they watch storms roll in, and the porch as a whole was arranged to welcome gatherings of friends and four generations of their family.

The upstairs porch, with its view of the pond, features a pair of rope hammocks made cozy with hand-stitched quilts. Jim and Dinah drop in to enjoy the peace and quiet after long days at their animal hospital with barking, mewing or neighing creatures. Jack and Jill, their frisky Chiweenies (of mixed Chihuahua and dachshund heritage) are welcome companions as the day draws to a close, but they are far from the only objects of the couple's affection. "We love this house so much," says Dinah, "that sometimes we just have to pet the logs!"

ABOVE: A Bybee Pottery spongewear planter adds a local dash of color on an old church pew.

CENTER: A birdhouse with its own little porch shelters the nest of winged friends.

RIGHT: Paired horseshoes are a nod to Kentucky's equine heritage.

OPPPOSITE: Frontier-era tools are displayed on the mule barn wall.

ABOVE: Local artist Doug Haley's spalted maple burl table and matching vases are all handcrafted and turned; the wood features the alluring, topographic dark streaks that race through the grain as a tree begins to decay. The striped tassel rug is by Dash & Albert.

RIGHT: A traditionally crafted broom rests against the joined poplar and oak logs.

FAR RIGHT: A vintage hickory slat chair stands beside a new hickory slat basket crafted by the artists of Berea College.

OPPOSITE: The Martins have a second, more private porch upstairs that looks onto the fishing pond out back. Their twin hammocks, softened by family quilts and down-filled pillows, are welcoming retreats at day's end. The cat's-paw rug is by Dash & Albert from Mulberry & Lime in Lexington.

A Painter's Porch

Katherine Sandoz and Daniel Bucey — Savannah, Georgia

Just a few miles north as the crow flies from the hectic buzz of Savannah's business district, the secluded rural neighborhood of artist Katherine Sandoz, her husband, Daniel Bucey, and their young sons, David and William, is enveloped by a symphony of cicadas. Shaded by a canopy of jungly magnolia trees and palmetto palms, the family's 1931 cypress bungalow has provided shelter from decades of heat and burdensome humidity.

Unlike many porches that are wide-open extensions of a yard with outward-facing benches, chairs and swings, this refuge is a continuation of the house. Katherine and Daniel furnished the space in a simple way that works equally well for dreaming, working, playing or dining; thanks to screening, the porch is ideally suited for all of these activities throughout much of the year. As an added bonus, cypress wood is naturally bug and moisture resistant. Sienna faux-silk dupioni curtains at either end extend the feeling of being in an interior space and help to keep out the sun or the rain when it's blown in sideways; the fabric doesn't sun-bleach, stain or mildew, as natural silk would.

Together with the privacy the curtains supply, the eight-foot porch depth promotes real intimacy. The presence of a substantial wooden chest of drawers and a sinuous iron table illustrates

LEFT: On Katherine's porch, "tools of the trade" double as atmospheric jewels.

OPPOSITE: A work in progress stands on a wooden easel with a view of the trees. Machine-washable faux-silk dupioni curtains offer privacy and relief from the sun's glare.

how the family have taken the practical language of interior design and transplanted it just beyond the walls. "It's more of an outdoor room than anything else," Katherine notes.

While relishing the comforts of the furniture, she's clearly inspired by the beauty from the lawn beyond: one bowl brims with pears, another cradles satin-skinned mushrooms that cropped up after a summer downpour, and a mason jar holds a cluster of creamy magnolia blossoms. The porch is a family room, but also serves as a studio for Katherine; stacked canvases, brushes in vases and a basketful of paint tubes all stand at the ready, while finished works adorn the clapboard walls.

From the cushioned iron chairs that Katherine perches on while sketching or sewing, a neighbor's grazing horses and Ossabaw Island mule can be viewed while the family's Labradors stay in close attendance. Daniel's white-tailed deer skull and antlers add a gentleman's touch and another reminder of the natural world just past the porch's bounds. In the fauna as well as the swaying fronds of the Boston ferns and the gentle nod of elephant's ears that line the path to their door (which grow as they will, rather than following any gardener's plans for symmetry), Katherine observes the ever-present hand of God. In this shady corner of the world, one needn't ask for more.

BELOW: Katherine's sketchbook and pencils are a still life all their own. The green etched glass, made from a recycled beer bottle, is by Marissa Drake; available from ShopSCAD.

BOTTOM: The family's Ophir English Labradors, Kirby and Boris, welcome guests to the bungalow. Ceramic planters hold a host of thriving plants; the yarn wreath is by Katie Runnels.

OPPOSITE: A white-tailed deer skull, landscape paintings and a vase full of camellias all speak to the couple's passions. The embroidered pillow is by Working Class Studio, the tablecloth is by Dani Niedzielski and the rug of renewable and recyclable interlocked "tiles" is by FLOR.

A Woodshed Porch

JOAN AND JERRY OPPENHEIMER — BRIDGEWATER, VERMONT

A woodshed isn't the most obvious setting for summertime breakfasts or winter evenings warmed by vintage quilts and a crackling fire; a transformative vision is required to convert such a utilitarian environment into a versatile living space. Joan and Jerry Oppenheimer's woodshed porch has the requisite rustic construction and cords of stacked firewood, but within the 600-square-foot area there are also a brick hearth, red-stained wicker seating and other vintage treasures that create intimate spaces for dining, reading, dozing and gazing.

Joan's grandparents purchased the property, an old dairy farm they named Coniston, in the 1930s and transformed it into a summer getaway. As Joan and Jerry approached retirement after decades of enjoying this home away from home, they hired local

LEFT: The American flag hangs outside the porch's entrance except during the winter holidays, when a beribboned holiday wreath is featured. The harsh Vermont winds and rains tatter the flag, so it must be "respectfully retired" every few years. The perennial phlox "Bright Eyes" at right is an heirloom plant, brought to the farm in the 1940s from Joan's grandparents' garden in Philadelphia. It was shared with Joan and Jerry when they landscaped their home fifty years later.

OPPOSITE: Snowshoes, old farm tools and checkerboards decorate the mantel in this woodshed, which was newly constructed to appear as if it had been a part of the environment for generations, like its sister porch down the hill. Darby, the Oppenheimers' Labrador retriever, looks on.

architect David Beilman to design their new residence on 45 acres of the farm. They didn't have to go far for their inspiration for the new porch: the woodshed attached to the nineteenth-century farmhouse down the hill had already been converted by Joan's family into a living space, complete with its own fireplace and wide barn doors opening onto verdant views.

It was Joan's mother who suggested the new site. Decades ago, as a young woman exploring the farm, she often returned

ABOVE: Coniston is the name given to the farm by Joan's grandparents; the couple's 45-acre property within its bounds is affectionately named The Gravel Pit, because its pond was formed from one such pit. In cold or inclement weather, glass doors are raised from the basement to insulate the open doorways. The side table is formed from an old sewing machine's base and a vintage game board.

to a crest of the hayfield to look east toward the New Hampshire mountains. Once morning mist has lifted from the rolling slopes painted in soft shades of blue and green, the view extends for miles. At day's end, orange and lilac hues spread over the forested land.

In 1997, Joan and Jerry broke ground in an immature spruce grove at the edge of the hayfield. The woodshed is positioned midway between the barn and home, connecting the three and thus serving as a true indoor/outdoor space. "We wanted our home to

recede into the scenery, not compete with it," Jerry explains, and so they selected unpainted locally milled spruce and pine along with weathered antique boards for construction for the porch. Left untreated, the softwood floor welcomes muddy boots and dogs alike.

Furnishings hail from flea markets and antique stores, lending a lived-in look enhanced by funky finds like an old wooden ironing board that supports a Boston fern. A vintage game board tops a cast-iron sewing machine base to form a side table, while a wooden cake pedestal showcases an arrangement of pomegranates and bittersweet branches.

What had once been a working farm and, later, a summer respite, has become the couple's (and Joan's mother's) year-round residence, offering four seasons of unique delights. In autumn, the family presses wild apples from the property into cider as the mountains blaze with the region's famous fall color from the ash, birch, beech and maple trees. Later in the year, the family watches from their hearth-warmed seats through the paned glass pocket doors as snowdrifts and icicles set the stage for cardinals, mink and moose, and for children and grandchildren at play on the hills and frozen pond.

Soon enough, cherry blossoms flutter to the ground and several thousand daffodils push their sunny blooms up through the soil. Spring arrives so fast, Jerry notes, that "all of a sudden, what was just a bunch of sticks becomes leaves." And, finally, in summer—cool starry nights filled with fireflies follow warm days with the occasional bear climbing a cherry tree for a treat. The glass doors, inspired by those found at Monticello, roll back down into the basement to let in the fresh air during warm stretches, creating a nice crosscurrent when the front barn door is open.

Coming from hectic and demanding professional and social lives in Washington, D.C., Joan and Jerry have embraced both the remote property and its peaceful traditions. Five generations of their family have enjoyed the pageants of passing seasons from the woodshed porches; their care of the land and thoughtful construction help assure that the next five generations will cherish it, too.

BELOW: Breakfast and other informal meals are shared on the porch.

OPPOSITE: Red wicker adds a splash of color to the locally milled spruce and pine; quilts and vintage rugs soften the atmosphere of the untreated wood.

An Australian Veranda in Sonoma County

LINDA AND TOMMY DeHENNIS — GLEN ELLEN, CALIFORNIA

San Franciscan Linda DeHennis was looking for an alternate way home from Sonoma County when she happened upon a section of road that brought Australia to mind. Having traveled to that continent in the late 1980s on a life-altering adventure that included a two-week solo walkabout, her eye was drawn to the rolling eucalyptus-dotted hills. Coincidentally, at that time she was considering locations for a weekend home in the country; after further exploration, the neighboring town of Glen Ellen suited her perfectly with its charm and unpretentious air. Within a few years, Linda had purchased property along a creek, and designed and constructed this sprawling house, which stood ready to greet her and her new husband, Tommy. The home offers them respite from their city life paired with the look and comforts of the residences she had established in Victoria over many years of long-term stays in Australia.

LEFT: The guest cottage was the first house built on the property; its materials, including eucalyptus logs and corrugated steel sheets, are meant to be more humble and less "finished" than those of the main residence.

OPPOSITE: A vintage iron bed from Adelaide (foreground) is a perfect napping spot with a pillow hand-knitted by Linda. The bathtub is an adapted aluminum horse trough. The porch sconces over the tub were designed by Jim Misner using an old tap and die toolbox for back plates, vintage pressure gauges and mercury glass shades.

A deep veranda fully wraps the 7,500-square-foot "station," or ranch house. The exterior's visible joist construction is referred to as "inside out" and is typical of an outback homestead house, but the architectural detailing as a whole borrows elements from across the continent. "It's a conglomeration," Linda explains. "It captures the spirit of the place with particular aspects brought in, like the steel roof, the exposed joists, the wrapping porch, the fireplaces at both ends and how the whole structure is raised to catch the breeze."

Working with Australian architect Michael Rigg and San Francisco–based project architect Shawn Montoya, Linda designed a home that's rich with unique accents inside and out, including imported jarrah eucalyptus and Huon pine paneling, custom-designed furniture and lighting fixtures and original works of art. The emotional element of her vision was formed in part by the memory of her grandmother's home on Lake Mohawk in New Jersey. "My sister and I spent every summer on her jalousie-windowed porch," Linda reminisces. "We were always happy to be there and eager to return."

A number of "rooms" around all four sides of the house make it easy to live out

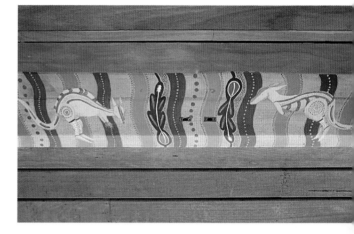

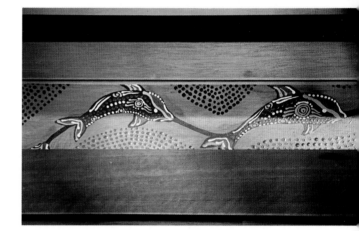

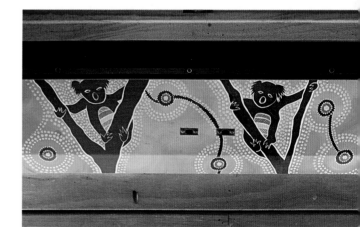

RIGHT: Aboriginal-painting-inspired thresholds at all fifteen doorways are a preview of coming attractions inside; each features a different motif.

OPPOSITE: Jim Misner's steel pendant lamp incorporates two crystal prisms from Linda's grandmother's chandelier. The crossed cables seen in the screened window are part of the earthquake-proofing of the home; the retractable screens keep wasps and other insects away when dinner is being served.

in the fresh Sonoma air. A dining area with retractable screens and tandem wicker sofas arranged in front of a fireplace invites leisurely entertaining, while another screened area features a vintage cast-iron napping bed and aluminum bathtub, with views of the more rustic guest cottage for solitary rejuvenation. The 258-foot expanse of walls—even as interrupted by scores of windows and doors—offers ample space for what could be called a sheltered gallery, which displays an eclectic mix of weather-resistant Australian treasures, some of aboriginal design and other vintage finds.

Linda lived in the guest cottage behind the house when the main home was under construction; it, too, has a screened "sleep out" porch at back and an open porch wrapping two other sides. "The smaller house, as the story goes in my imagination, was the ranchers' first home, while the main house was built after the farming went well and they could afford more space and luxuries," she says. The materials for the cottage are therefore less refined, with an exterior of stripped bark eucalyptus logs and rusted corrugated

ABOVE LEFT: With hundreds of feet of wall space, the veranda offers room for displaying antiques and works of art. Here, vintage river level markers from Sydney add a strikingly graphic presence to the serene exterior. An aboriginal snake sculpture slithers across the decking.

ABOVE RIGHT: A tin kangaroo from Broken Hill, New South Wales, rests in front of a blind door cupboard with a rope knot pull that keeps extra chairs and lawn games out of sight.

metal sheets on the roof and sides. The furnishings are a bit more "higgly piggly" as Linda puts it, too, slightly mismatched and funky, but with a welcoming character all their own.

Linda's bi-hemispheric life continues as she and her husband travel at each equinox to the far sides of the world, but in between, she's glad to have this Glen Ellen home as a refuge. "I have to pinch myself sometimes—it's hard to believe my vision for it was realized so beautifully," she shares. "It's as if this house were living inside of me for fifteen years until it finally burbled out."

BELOW: The corrugated-steel roof had to be treated with flat paints to reduce the glare that had posed a threat to both birds and aircraft overhead. Steel rainwater tanks line the front of the home; they can be used for gardening as well as for emergencies in this drought- and fire-prone area. A eucalyptus-leaf theme runs throughout the property, as evidenced by the large silver weather vane that crowns the roof, the shade of silvery green used for the exterior paneling, marquetry detailing the billiards room and curtains with damask leaf patterns.

CREATING
PORCH ROOMS

Bringing a Porch to Light

Furnishing Your Nest

Adding Color and Comfort with Textiles

Designer Michael Pelkey's board-and-batten cottage in Key West, Florida, was likely a home to cigar factory workers or spongers. In keeping with this informal past, Michael created a warm welcome with weathered rushed rockers and coral-filled English urns.

Bringing a Porch to Light

On theater stages, lighting is a formative and magical element that engages the audience, fostering the suspension of disbelief. In the same fashion, functional and fanciful lighting works its magic on the porch by enhancing whatever action takes place there. Illuminating a porch for evening use adds an emotional charge to all gatherings and extends the hours that it can serve as an outdoor room.

Outdoor lights can function as stage props that highlight the history, location and theme of a home. An iron lantern hanging from a sturdy chain brings quaint charm to the front porch of a weathered farmhouse. Playful strings of twinkling white lights can outline arches and unique architectural details, adding year-round star power even to traditional homes. Pillar candles set in large glass cylinders, embedded in sand or surrounded by seashells and driftwood bring everyday sea treasures to a beach house porch as well as a gentle flickering glow.

Porch lighting ought to be soft and romantic, not harsh or jarring. With today's variety of fixtures in color, shape and materials,

LEFT: A ceramic tiki frog is an unusual and festive welcome at a Palm Beach home designed by Lori Deeds for Kemble Interiors.

OPPOSITE: At the same home, a variety of light fixtures—including vintage metal lemon trees on the walls, hurricane candles and a pineapple-shaped table lit from within by candles—all add to the glow. The pineapple table is part of the Palm Beach collection by Mimi McMakin and Brooke Huttig of Kemble Interiors for Laneventure.

lighting serves as a medium for personal expression. Hanging lanterns and fairy-tale votive candles in trees evoke an enchanted forest, whereas the clean lines of modern fixtures signal urban sophistication. While the creative possibilities are endless, functional and practical elements should be considered before beginning any outdoor lighting project. As form follows function, give careful thought to how the space will ultimately be used—including its relation to the house and the surrounding environment. How will the porch be incorporated into a daily lifestyle? Will it serve as a sanctuary, candlelit for solitary reflection, or as a family gathering space bright enough to keep an eye on the children?

As in real estate, "location, location, location" is the key to successful porch lighting. Avoid harsh (and unflattering) overhead lighting, which can also interfere with the view. Instead, position canister lights behind planters to create leafy shadows of foliage and soft, glowing corners or incorporate recessed lighting into the floors to uplight the space. Dimmer switches can reduce glare and modulate mood, just as they do inside your home. For brighter spaces, place weatherproof table and floor lamps near chairs and sofas to transform porches into after-hours reading nooks or study spaces. Filigreed metal lanterns and candles create an ambience perfect for storytelling, watching fireflies and listening to crickets. Encase

ABOVE AND LEFT: Jim Misner's custom-designed lighting sculptures (as seen at the DeHennis home) are eclectic alternatives to off-the-shelf fixtures.

candles in lanterns or hurricane shades to avoid having to frequently relight them. Candles should always be weighted and secure to stay put on windy evenings. Or consider flickering LED lights as candle substitutes, especially if children or pets are underfoot.

Location and climate dictate practical considerations, especially in areas prone to extreme weather. Lamp casing materials react specifically to exposure. Without lacquer, copper and bronze acquire a patina over time. Ferrous metals such as iron and steel will rust, while stainless steel and aluminum stay pristine for years. Weatherproof lamp shades, in solution-dyed acrylic fabrics, are available in a full spectrum of colors and the latest prints and patterns to add texture and complement inside decor. While exterior-specific lighting is becoming more commonplace, double-check lights for outdoor safety. The Underwriters Laboratory (UL) sticker should guarantee lights are suitable for damp climates.

In recent years, many manufacturers have jumped on the outdoor lighting bandwagon, ensuring that almost any look, from period-perfect historical replicas to exotic themes and sleek ultra modern styles, is readily available. Creative shoppers also scour flea markets and antique shops for everything from vintage kerosene hurricane lamps to unique items to reuse as a lamp base or candle stand. For illumination inspiration, observe architecture, art, trends in home embellishments, and of course, always spend time in nature. Lighting, like all design elements, is a highly personal choice. Beyond the latest trends, or most elaborate fixtures, perfect lighting attracts people, complements surroundings and creates festive environments.

ABOVE: Gas lamps from Bevolo Gas Lights in New Orleans add period ambience to the Reynoldses' Queen Anne home in Point Clear, Alabama.

CENTER: A traditional mission slag-glass light casts an amber glow onto the redwood shingles of Bea Bowles's Craftsman cottage in San Francisco, California.

RIGHT: A cast-iron pineapple sconce by Kemble Interiors for Laneventure creates playful shadows through its pierced shell, at a Palm Beach, Florida, home.

Furnishing Your Nest

Rather than serving simply as a passage from indoors to out, the porch can be a welcoming living space for many activities. Furnishings create comfortable nooks and cozy settings that signal visitors to slow down, relax and take a breather from the everyday hustle and bustle of life. Porch furniture evokes retreat and respite, and it can serve as theater-style seating for nature's seasonal spectacles. But it can also make a statement: your porch is the first or final expression of style your home makes. The right seating and accent pieces (along with well-chosen textiles and lighting) create a welcoming committee that sets the mood for you and your guests.

Outdoor furniture hasn't always been this desirable or even acceptable, as its popularity has ebbed and flowed. Porch furniture reflects changes in American history, industry and social patterns. Nineteenth-century porches were often the center of social life, where, weather permitting, neighbors gathered to eat, drink and tell tall tales. Seating, basic and essential, ranged

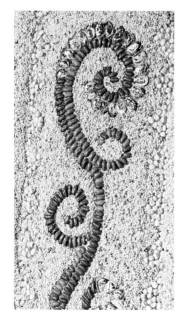

LEFT: Dried corn, peas and a variety of seeds were used as the artist's materials for one of a hundred salvaged doors decorated for a charity auction in Lexington, Kentucky.

OPPOSITE: At the home of Becky and Reese Reinhold in Lexington, a French country farm table from Belle Maison Antiques creates an outdoor dining room with a view of old-growth trees. The glass lamp is by Arteriors; the Ripple vases are by Shiraleah; both are from Mulberry & Lime.

from the handmade wooden or cane chairs of rural dwellers to the fancier wicker and rattan of the leisure class.

Architect Clem Schaub notes that the trend in outdoor living is such that porches are increasingly taking on the dimensions of interior rooms, so that conversational and dining areas can be established. "We're moving away from the 'deck of the ship' problem, where people are looking out on a scene but not at each other," he says. Outdoor kitchens and fireplaces are also increasingly incorporated, helping to create what he calls "living porches." In addition, manufacturers have responded to the call for greater variety and more durable materials, providing a vast array of new furnishings that add comfort and creativity to any porch. While wicker and rattan pieces remain traditional favorites, synthetic versions are increasingly replacing the natural materials that break down easily when left to the elements. New surface treatments for aluminum and stainless steel frames such as powder coating reduce wear and tear and extend life span. Paired with an array of all-weather cushions, these pieces can be comfortable and stylish additions to porches of all types. More durable materials enable designers to ramp up styling, creating living possibilities as limitless as the imagination.

The rocking chair, an early must-have piece, is an enduring American icon, associated with presidents from Lincoln to Kennedy and literary lions like Mark Twain and Joel Chandler Harris. The porch swing, indigenous to the South, is similarly evocative. It conjures up cool breezes and iced tea on hot summer afternoons, or couples holding hands while watching fireflies

ABOVE: A willow twig chair is as sculptural as it is functional.

CENTER: A midcentury butterfly chair at the Philo Apple Farm is a relaxed and modern addition to a guest cottage porch.

LEFT: A true all-weather piece, a vintage cast-metal garden chair at the Hemingway Home in Key West, Florida, adds graceful curves to the porch.

light up the gloaming. Rocking chairs and swings evolved into midcentury bouncer chairs and gliders that allow gentle motion. They're also more portable than swings, and offer more access to tables laden with food or drink.

Climate and travel influenced the popularity of sleeping porches, especially in Victorian homes. Sleeping porches, in all shapes and sizes, offered cool accommodations for visiting family members, traveling salesmen or wealthy Northerners on overnight train stops en route to winter in Palm Beach, Florida. The Aiken sofa, a grandiose piece with a large mattress, was created in Aiken, South Carolina, for these wayfarers, and has evolved into today's outdoor sofa beds that double as seating during the day (or even a space for a nap or two).

The advent of air-conditioning in the mid-twentieth century sent people indoors to marvel at miraculous climate-controlled interiors. From the fifties to the mideighties, outdoor spaces were ignored, according to John Danzer, a self-proclaimed "exterior decorator," and president of Munder-Skiles, a New York manufacturer of luxury outdoor furniture. "A picnic table or a swing set for the kids was about it," says Danzer. "Even twenty years ago, there was no level of sophistication in porch furniture. Since then, when designers began creating fantasy outdoor spaces like those at Miami's Delano Hotel, suddenly everybody wanted similar outdoor worlds at home."

Danzer advocates a functional, less-is-more approach, and careful consideration of the porch's stylistic connection to the house. Ultramodern boxy sofas and aluminum fixtures on the porch of a traditional Georgian house probably won't work, just as Rococo pieces on a Craftsman bungalow porch may provide a similar shock.

Consider incorporating portable metamorphic pieces, such as small folding tables, nesting ottomans or hammocks that can be easily changed with moods, or completely removed to open up space. "Furnishing today's porches is like decorating a loft," said Danzer. "Whatever the space, from rustic to grand, the porch should be a true living space, where almost any activity can comfortably take place."

BELOW: A nineteenth-century French marble-topped baker's table at the Parker home in Savannah, Georgia, also serves as a supper table for the family.

BOTTOM: The acid-stained concrete-topped "Scissor" table with induced rusted steel legs at the Philo Apple Farm was designed by Joe Bates for Fabrication; available from Furnishings for Friends.

OVERLEAF: At this elegant reconstructed barn home in Woodstock, Vermont, what was once the milking parlor is now a slate-floored screened porch with a welcoming set of cushioned wicker.

Adding Color and Comfort with Textiles

Even when unfurnished and unadorned, a porch is already awash in the colors and textures of nature. The view presents a drama of ever-shifting seasons: the buttery slant of an autumn sunset, the ice blue of winter's first snowfall, spring's rainbow bouquet of flowers and the emerald green of summer foliage. Incorporating fabrics into your porch's decor can reflect, enhance and complement nature's spectacles. Colorful cushions, pillows, curtains and accessories can all become instant mood-setters. Thanks to the latest fiber technologies, not only are high-performance textiles available in brilliant, highly saturated shades, but they are also treated to stay true to their shapes and colors, even when subjected to the elements.

New treatment techniques for outdoor fabrics help repel water, heat and ultraviolet light. Sunbrella, one of the original outdoor-friendly fabric companies, includes an acrylic undercoating that won't trap heat, allowing for cool, comfortable seating during the hottest Fourth of July porch picnic. Even when exposed to an unexpected afternoon storm, cushions will drain, if leaned upright against a wall, and be party-ready by that same evening. Many cushion seats include waterproof liners and antimicrobial treatments that resist mildew.

LEFT: A vintage chenille throw with a ribbon motif is paired with buttoned and folk-art pillows.

OPPOSITE: At Annette and Tim Grahl's home (and Scottwood Bed and Breakfast) in Midway, Kentucky, an Americana screened porch includes an array of new and vintage fabrics.

An increasing number of upscale fabric manufacturers now offer complete outdoor lines. Scalamandré's Island Cloth collection, Robert Allen's Portico collection and Perennials outdoor fabrics all offer a wide variety of choices. The new generation of fabrics allows items usually reserved for inside rooms to come out into the open air. Just as outdoor and indoor use has become interchangeable, fashion and home fabrics are increasingly intertwined. Home fabrics are up-to-the-minute reflections of the latest fashion trends, especially as designers from Ralph Lauren to Vera Wang offer home and fashion collections.

Outdoor cushions are no longer the rigid, stale-smelling canvas blocks that were just slightly more comfortable than church pews. Now, fabrics can be durable and feel as soft as sinking into a summer cloud. Pillows can be piled on, as these high-tech fabrics forever put an end to the need to lug indoor cushions outside.

Changing, rotating and adding new pillows is the easiest trick to bring a new look to a porch with minimal investment and no heavy lifting. While matching sets of monochromatic cushions

ABOVE LEFT: At the DeHennis home, woven reed sofas are softened by Ecuadorian pillows, a sheepskin throw and a vintage aboriginal fishing basket.

ABOVE RIGHT: At the Philo Apple Farm, hand-stitched pillows add color and a sense of play.

are still preferred by more traditional home owners, mixing things up offers a more modern look. Patterns, stripes, checks, swirls and florals live happily ever after on various porch pieces. New vintage-inspired creations, such as "Savannah Toile" fabric as well as all-weather pillows and even coordinating melamine plates (all from Working Class Studio), add jazz to any porch. Beyond cushions and pillows, fabrics can also add texture and color when used as tablecloths, throws, wall hangings, rugs and window treatments.

The newest outdoor fabrics require little maintenance, but minimal care goes a long way: shake cushions out frequently, especially during spring pollen season, and wipe down with a damp cloth. Some fabrics are machine-washable, but check labels for restrictions.

Outdoor rugs have evolved into works of art, simulating fine indoor Orientals or making contemporary statements for artistic yet playful appeal. Curtains, drapes and shades can offer privacy, color and a bit of mystery to a porch. Damask, jacquard and even treated velvet outdoor curtains make a dramatic statement, but be sure to use these luxurious fabrics in small doses to avoid a heavy, overly formal look. Summer dictates light, airy, treated gauze or faux linen hanging from ceiling hooks and billowing in the wind.

While technical advances and creative design have revolutionized outdoor living, the green movement has spurred new interest in eco-friendly, natural fibers. Manufacturers offer fabrics made from recycled materials, and popular new organics include flax, sea grass, bamboo and hemp—all treated for softness and durability.

For an eclectic, one-of-a-kind effect, favorite personal vintage pieces and family textiles can have new life. Create a porch gallery by transforming old fabrics into individual artistic expressions that are entirely one of a kind. Bring heirlooms out of cedar chests and closets for outdoor display. Antique quilts, tapestries, vintage doll clothes and needlepoint all add charm, warmth and color. Nautical flags, seaside striped umbrella cloth and sailing fabrics are natural accessories for beach porches. For textilelike color and pattern without the costs or care of fabric, use an old standby—deck paint—to create stripes, checkerboard or even polka-dot floors and walls.

BELOW: Appliquéd and beaded pillows are a sweet addition to Bea Bowles's Craftsman cottage in San Francisco.

Design Directory

Architects

Beilman Architecture
Bridgewater, Vermont
www.beilman.net
802-672-3323

Clark Graff
Fairlee, Vermont
802-333-9441

Clemens Bruns Schaub Architect and Associates
Vero Beach, Florida
www.clemensbrunsschaub.com
772-231-1484

Gale Garth Carroll
Corpus Christi, Texas
512-883-6821

Max Strang Architecture
Miami, Florida
www.strangarchitecture.com
305-373-4990

Montoya and Associates
Petaluma, California
www.montoya-associates.com
707-763-8006

Oppenheim Architecture + Design
Miami, Florida
www.oppenoffice.com
305-576-8404

Randolph Martz
Charleston, South Carolina
www.randolphmartz.com
843-722-1339

Smith & Vansant
Norwich, Vermont
www.smithandvansant.com
802-649-5515

Smith Architectural Group, Inc.
Palm Beach, Florida
www.smitharchitecturalgroup.com
561-832-0202

Thomas & Denzinger Architects
Charleston, South Carolina
www.thomasanddenzinger.com
843-723-6651

Walcott Adams Verneuille Architects
Fairhope, Alabama
www.wavarchitects.com
251-928-6041

Wellington Reiter
Principal, Urban Instruments, Inc.
312-608-0840

Artists and Designers

Archival Decor
www.archivaldecor.com
415-320-5977

Arteriors Home
www.arteriorshome.com
877-488-8866

Berea College Crafts
www.bereacollegecrafts.com
800-347-3892

Bybee Pottery
859-369-5350

Dash & Albert Rug Company
www.dashandalbert.com
800-658-5035

DwellStudio
www.dwellshop.com
877-99-DWELL

Enzo Enea
Enea Garden Design Inc.
www.enea-garden.ch
305-576-6702

FLOR
www.flor.com
866-281-3567

Matthew Foley
859-779-2202

Gorky Gonzalez
Gorky Pottery
www.gorkypottery.com

Doug Haley
Haley-Daniels Custom Furniture
www.haleydaniels.com
859-986-7243

Carolyn Young Hisel
Represented by Ann Tower Gallery
www.anntowergallery.com
859-425-1188

Jim Misner Light Designs
www.jimmisnerlightdesigns.com
415-928-0400

J Thomas Design
www.jthomasdesign.com

KleinReid
www.kleinreid.com
718-937-3828

Katie Runnels
www.theconstantgatherer.com
803-381-2052

Larry Young Sculpture
www.youngsculpture.com
573-449-6810

Ron Meece
Represented by Longitude Art
www.longitudeart.com
859-299-0914

Meryl Truett Photography
www.meryltruett.com
912-656-2270

Jesús Moroles
www.moroles.com

Simon Pearce
www.simonpearce.com
800-774-5277

Pol's Potten
www.polspotten.nl
020-4193541

Charles Ramberg
Ramberg Furniture
www.rambergfurniture.com
843-556-8550

Katherine Sandoz
www.katherinesandoz.com
912-596-3142

Eric Scholtens
Natural Forms Furniture
www.naturalformsfurniture.com
270-993-5983

Working Class Studio
www.workingclassstudio.com
912-525-6300

Furniture

Bielecky Brothers, Inc.
www.bieleckybrothers.com
212-753-2355

Christian Liaigre
www.christian-liaigre.fr
212-891-2500 and 312-644-1844

Fabrication
www.fabricationnapa.com
707-224-9057

Furnishings for Friends
www.furnishingsforfriends.com
707-224-9057

Laneventure
www.laneventure.com
800-235-3558

McGuire Furniture Company
www.mcguirefurniture.com

Pawleys Island Hammocks
www.hammockshop.com
800-332-3490

Summer Classics
www.summerclassics.com
888-868-4267

Sutherland Furniture
www.sutherlandfurniture.com
214-638-4161

Interior Designers

Margaret Moore Chambers
2 M Design
Atlanta, Georgia
917-620-5509

Lori Deeds
Kemble Interiors, Inc.
Palm Beach, Florida
www.kembleinteriors.com
561-659-5556

Erin Martin
Martin Showroom
St. Helena, California
www.martinshowroom.com
707-963-4141

Maria Molinari
Miami Lakes, Florida
www.mariafernandamolinari.com

Mary Morrow
2-Story Tree
San Francisco, California
www.2storytree.com
415-346-0362

Michael Pelkey
305-304-4870

Susie Rucker
Rucker & Rucker, Inc.
Corpus Christi, Texas
361-994-1231

Tom Scheerer Incorporated
New York, New York
www.tomscheerer.com
212-529-0744

Landscape Designers

Mac Reid and Tay Breene
Lexington, Kentucky
859-865-2160

Mario Nievera Design
New York, New York, and
Palm Beach, Florida
www.marionieveradesign.com
212-533-2683 and 561-659-2820

Robert Parsley
Miami, Florida
305-665-9688

Shops

Andrianna Shamaris
New York, New York, and Malibu, California
www.andriannashamaris.com
212-388-9898 and 310-456-2243

Arthur Roger Gallery
New Orleans, Louisiana
www.arthurrogergallery.com
504-522-1999

Belle Maison Antiques
Lexington, Kentucky
www.bellemaisonantiques.com
859-252-9030

Bevolo Gas and Electric Lights
New Orleans, Louisiana
www.bevolo.com
504-522-9485

Circa Lighting
Savannah, Georgia
www.circalighting.com
877-762-2323

Crocker Antiques and Garden
Fairhope, Alabama
251-990-9355

The Farmhouse Mercantile
Boonville, California
707-895-3996

Martin Showroom
St. Helena, California
www.martinshowroom.com
707-967-8787

Mulberry & Lime
Lexington, Kentucky
www.mulberryandlime.com
859-231-0800

Odegard
Miami, Florida
www.odegardinc.com
305-576-7166

The Paris Market & Brocante
Savannah, Georgia
www.theparismarket.com
912-232-1500

ShopSCAD
Savannah, Georgia
www.shopscadonline.com
912-525-5180

Textiles

While many textile companies supply material only to the trade, the Web sites and phone number below offer a look into the styles available.

Bassett McNab Company
267-508-0001

Donghia
www.donghia.com

Duralee
www.duralee.com

John Hutton
www.johnhutton.com

Perennials
www.perennialsfabrics.com

Scalamandré
www.scalamandre.com

Sunbrella
www.sunbrella.com

Index

Dedicated with love to my sister, Pamela E. Rhame —P.S.W.

Acknowledgments

The quest for these porches led us from south to north and east to west. A host of hospitable and knowledgeable individuals paved the way throughout the towns, cities and states we've been fortunate to explore. We would like to thank the following friends and colleagues for their generosity: Martha von Ammon, Tay Breene and Mac Reid, Jon Carloftis, Julie Cauthen, Laurie Chester, Paula Danyluk, Eleanore De Sole, Lulu DeVeer, Julie Dorman, Rebecca Dykes, Freddi Evans, Donna Goldfein, John Goldthwait, David Gonzales, Annette Grahl, Demi Bowles Lathrop, Mary Marcom, Jim Misner, Barry Moser, Marc Nadel, Marty and Dennis Roderick, Barbie Tafel Thomas, Stephanie Grider Tittle, Doug Ulwick, Lea Verneuille, Malcolm White, and Denise Whiting. We would also like to thank the team at Random House for their collective expertise and support: Editorial Director Doris Cooper, Production Manager Joan Denman, Editor Aliza Fogelson, Editorial Assistant Peggy Paul, Publisher Lauren Shakely, Designer Amy Sly, Production Editor Christine Tanigawa and Art Director Jane Treuhaft.

Published in the United States by Clarkson Potter/Publishers, an imprint of the Crown Publishing Group, a division of Random House, Inc., New York.
www.crownpublishing.com
www.clarksonpotter.com

Clarkson Potter is a trademark and Potter with colophon is a registered trademark of Random House, Inc.

Library of Congress Cataloging-in-Publication Data is available upon request.

ISBN 978-0-307-46024-0
Printed in China

Packaged by Design Press, a division of Savannah College of Art and Design
www.designpressbooks.com
www.scad.edu

SCAD Creative Team

Creative Director: Anna Marlis Burgard
Designers: Matthew Cole and Angela Rojas
Editors: Alexis Barnes, Craig Kellogg, Harrison Key and Georgia Lee
Photographers: Chia Chong (Alabama, California, Florida, Georgia, Kentucky, Mississippi and Vermont) and Adam Kuehl
    (Georgia, Massachusetts, Mississippi, South Carolina and Texas)
Photographer's Assistant: Jonathan Moore (California and Georgia)
Stylists: Trish Andersen (California), Wendy Anderson (Vermont), David Busch (Florida), Rebecca Gardner (Alabama, Florida,
    Georgia, Mississippi and Texas) and Amy Zurcher (Georgia and Kentucky)

10 9 8 7 6 5 4 3 2 1
First Edition